4,95

THE SIOUX UPRISING of 1862

THE SIOUX UPRISING of 1862

KENNETH CARLEY

THE MINNESOTA HISTORICAL SOCIETY · ST. PAUL · 1976

© 1961, 1976 BY THE MINNESOTA HISTORICAL SOCIETY, ST. PAUL 55101

SECOND EDITION

10   9   8   7   6   5   4   3

Library of Congress Cataloging in Publication Data
Carley, Kenneth.
  The Sioux uprising of 1862.
  (Publications of the Minnesota Historical Society)
  Bibliography: p.
  Includes index.
  1. Dakota Indians — Wars, 1862-1865. I. Title. II.
Series: Minnesota Historical Society. Publications.
E83.86.C37   1976   977.6'04   76-16499

International Standard Book Number:
0-87351-103-4 paper cover

PREFACE

THIS BOOK, like the first edition published in 1961, attempts to present an accurate, concise narrative in words and pictures of the Sioux Uprising of 1862 in Minnesota. The second edition is an amplification of its predecessor in terms of text, pictures, and, in a few instances, interpretation. Two wholly new chapters, as well as numerous illustrations, have been added, and the entire text has been carefully reviewed and revised in the light of recently discovered source materials and the research of other scholars since 1961. The two new sections deal with the lengthy siege of Fort Abercrombie — a related episode distant from the main arena in the Minnesota River Valley — and with the "Banishment from Minnesota" — the often sad experiences of the various splinters of the Sioux or Dakota peoples after the uprising. Throughout the book a special effort has been made to incorporate material which sheds light on the Sioux side of the story, and the greatly enlarged text of chapter 10 now also discusses the Chippewa disturbance of 1862, which was quelled before it could spread warfare throughout the entire state. Almost all chapters now offer more information than did the earlier edition.

Although the main body of pictures has been kept, some have been added. Among new ones to surface since the first edition is a portrait of Andrew J. Myrick, a trader hated by the Indians. Efforts were made to identify every picture reproduced here, and available information has been included. If a photograph is not dated or otherwise fully identified, it is because that information could not be located. Credit lines accompany each picture and give its source if it is not in the Minnesota Historical Society's collection. All illustrations without such credits are from the voluminous files of the society's audio-visual library. The drawing on the title page is an authentic Sioux design in a typical geometric pattern favored by that tribe.

Anyone retelling the story of events that took place more than a century ago is, of course, indebted to earlier writers, especially to those survivors who left accounts of their frequently harrowing experiences. A record of the principal works consulted appears at the end of the book in an expanded "List of Sources." But these witnesses, many of whom did not set down their reminiscences until several decades later, as well as historians who have since studied the events, disagree so frequently about seemingly obvious details that it has been necessary to resolve conflicting testimony at every turn. In some cases it has not been possible to do this satisfactorily, and the author willingly assumes responsibility for any errors and for his conclusions on the numerous controversial aspects of this major frontier war.

Many people have helped in the production of the two editions of this book, and the author herewith expresses his gratitude to all of them. He wants especially to thank Nancy Eubank, interpretation supervisor of the Minnesota Historical Society's field services, historic sites, and archaeology division, for her many helpful suggestions and leads to material for the new edition. Among other things, Ms. Eubank was responsible for the development of the informative exhibits in the society's interpretive centers at the Lower Sioux Agency and Fort Ridgely. From these the author is pleased to use the carefully researched drawings by staff artists Chester Kozlak and Paul Waller. Archaeological reports by David Nystuen, Gordon A. Lothson, and Loren C. Johnson on excavations at the Lower and Upper Sioux agencies and Fort Ridgely were also helpful. Donn Coddington, head of the historic sites division, and Alan R. Woolworth, chief of archaeology, readily lent assistance whenever the author asked for it.

The chapter on New Ulm owes much to the expert help of Mrs. Leota M. Kellett, former director of the Brown County Historical Society. Her successor, Paul Klammer, also kindly answered queries for the new edition. The late Willoughby M. Babcock, former curator of newspapers in the Minnesota Historical Society, gave generously of his knowledge of the Sioux and the Minnesota Valley. Among the author's fellow members of the Twin Cities Civil War Round Table who offered helpful criticism or companionship on travels to uprising sites were Wallace J. Schutz, Leo J. Ambrose, Rodney C. Loehr, William H. Rowe, and Richard B. Dunsworth. My wife, Lucile, read each chapter in its numerous versions and suggested alterations from the viewpoint of a general reader.

For their part in the preparation of this volume, the author wishes to thank colleagues in the Minnesota Historical Society's division of archives and manuscripts and the newspaper and reference departments of the library. He is especially grateful for the assistance of Lila J. Goff, Bonnie Wilson, and Eugene D. Becker (who took pictures and prepared prints for publication) of the audio-visual library. Above all, he wants to thank June D. Holmquist, assistant director for research and publications, and Jean A. Brookins, managing editor. Mrs. Holmquist's expert editing in all phases did much to shape the final product. The author is also grateful to Alan Ominsky, production supervisor, for the book's handsome design and maps.

Finally, the author wishes to acknowledge the sabbatical leave that provided the uninterrupted time needed to prepare this new edition. The respite from his regular duties as editor of *Minnesota History* was made possible by the society's Charles E. Flandrau Research Fund dedicated under the terms of Mrs. Grace Flandrau's will to finance staff research. It is especially fitting that the man for whom the fund is named played a leading role in the events described in these pages.

When the first edition of this book appeared, its publication was aided by the Louis W. and Maud Hill Family Foundation, now the Northwest Area Foundation, of St. Paul. *The Sioux Uprising of 1862* was the first book to be published from a revolving fund established for the society by the foundation in 1961. Over the years the fund has continued to fulfill its grantors' intentions, revolving again and again to swell a growing list of studies on various aspects of the heritage of the Northwest. It is our sincere hope that the second edition will make a small contribution to the continuing interpretation of that heritage.

St. Paul   *Kenneth Carley*
August 1, 1976

CHRONOLOGY OF THE 1862 UPRISING

AUGUST 17, 1862

Murder of five settlers at Acton in Meeker County

AUGUST 18, 1862

Attacks on Upper and Lower Sioux agencies, other settlements, and the ambush at Redwood Ferry; beginning of Chippewa disturbance at Gull Lake

AUGUST 19, 1862

First attack on New Ulm; Sibley appointed to command volunteer troops

AUGUST 20, 1862

First attack on Fort Ridgely; attacks on the Lake Shetek and West Lake settlements

AUGUST 22, 1862

Main attack on Fort Ridgely

AUGUST 23, 1862

Second attack on New Ulm

SEPTEMBER 2, 1862

Battle of Birch Coulee

SEPTEMBER 3, 1862

Skirmish at Acton and attack on Fort Abercrombie

SEPTEMBER 4, 1862

Attacks on Forest City and Hutchinson

SEPTEMBER 6, 1862

Second attack on Fort Abercrombie

SEPTEMBER 23, 1862

Battle of Wood Lake

SEPTEMBER 26, 1862

Surrender of captives at Camp Release

SEPTEMBER 28, 1862

Military commission appointed to try Indians who participated in the uprising

DECEMBER 26, 1862

Thirty-eight Sioux executed at Mankato

CONTENTS

CHIEF LITTLE CROW. Drawing by Frank B. Mayer at Traverse des Sioux, July 2, 1851. Newberry Library.

I.
Causes of the Sioux Uprising

THE CIVIL WAR had drained Minnesota's energies and manpower for sixteen months when in August, 1862, the four-year-old state became embroiled in a second war within a war in its own back yard.

From their reservations along the upper Minnesota River, the proud Native Americans known as the Dakota or Sioux Indians, under the leadership of Chief Little Crow, rose to take the settlers in the Minnesota Valley by surprise. Before the Sioux Uprising (or the Dakota or Sioux War, as it is sometimes called) could be brought under control, at least 450 — and perhaps as many as 800 — white settlers and soldiers were killed, and considerable property was destroyed in southern Minnesota. Measured in terms of the number of civilian lives lost, the outbreak was one of the worst in American history, and it launched a series of Indian wars on the northern plains that did not end until 1890 with the battle of Wounded Knee in South Dakota.*

*The correct name of this Native American nation is Dakota, meaning "friends" or "allies." Sioux is a contraction of Nadouessioux (meaning "snake" or "snakelike enemy"), a name originally given them by their enemies, the Chippewa (or Ojibway). This term is, however, so widely used and so deeply entrenched in the literature of the 1862 uprising that no attempt has been made to avoid it in this text.

The exact number of dead in the war will never be known. The most thorough student of uprising casualties, Marion P. Satterlee, a Minneapolis newspaperman, arrived at a figure of 447 whites, civilian and military, in his final list compiled in 1919. Assuming that Satterlee missed some, the figure of 500 once offered by Governor Alexander Ramsey seems a good estimate. Since the Indians always tried to carry away or conceal their dead, we have no clear idea of Sioux losses. Later testimony by Indians indicated a total of twenty-one Dakota dead in various battles.

THE SITE *of the arbor where the treaty was signed in 1851 is marked by a plaque on this boulder in Traverse des Sioux State Park north of St. Peter. The pioneer log cabin was moved there in 1931 from a Nicollet County farm. The cabin is said to resemble one put up by trader Louis Provençalle, who ran a fur station in the area in the 1820s.*

What caused the 1862 uprising on the Minnesota frontier? The answer lies in a complex of reasons, some stemming from past events and some immediate and peculiar to the time. In the broadest sense, the war of 1862 was a small segment of the Sioux's long history of conflict, first with other Indian tribes and then with the white man. As far back as the seventeenth century, the Minnesota Sioux had been engaged in almost constant warfare with their traditional enemies, the Chippewa. Pressure from the Chippewa, who may have had more and better guns, perhaps coupled with the increased availability of horses and the prospect of a new life on the prairies, drew the Dakota gradually from the northern lakes and forests into the Big Woods and onto the prairies of the Minnesota Valley. There the white man found them.

During the nineteenth century, westward-moving settlers and their government further compressed the Sioux domain through a series of treaties, the most important of which were signed in 1851 at Traverse des Sioux and Mendota. On July 23, 1851, the Wahpeton and Sisseton bands of the Upper Sioux ceded to the United States their lands in southern and western Minnesota Territory, as well as some in Iowa and Dakota. The price for this magnificent empire was $1,665,000 in cash and annuities. On August 5 at Mendota the Mdewakanton and Wahpekute bands of Lower Sioux signed away their lands, which embraced most of the area in the southeast quarter of present-day Minnesota. For this, the government was to pay $1,410,000 in cash and annuities over a fifty-year period.

In all, the Sioux ceded almost 24,000,000 acres of rich agricultural

THE SIGNING *of the treaty of Traverse des Sioux in 1851 gave the United States possession of a vast area in southern Minnesota. Thirty-five Upper Sioux chiefs stepped forward to touch the pen in a colorful ceremony under a canopy of boughs.* OIL BY FRANCIS D. MILLET IN THE MINNESOTA CAPITOL.

land, which was legally opened to white settlement three years later. The treaties left these Indians — numbering some seven thousand — two reservations, each twenty miles wide and about seventy miles long, bordering the upper Minnesota River. There the federal government established two administrative centers known as the Upper (or Yellow Medicine) and Lower (or Redwood) agencies. That serving the Upper Sioux was placed near the mouth of the Yellow Medicine River below present-day Granite Falls, while the Lower Sioux Agency was erected about thirty miles down the Minnesota near what is now Redwood Falls.

The Upper Sioux considered the land assigned them—from Lake Traverse to the Yellow Medicine River—acceptable as a reservation, since it included the sites of their old villages. The Lower Sioux, however, voiced some dissatisfaction with their new domain, which stretched from the Yellow Medicine some sixty miles down the Minnesota River to Little Rock Creek about eight miles northwest of present-day New Ulm. The reserve was on the prairie, far from their favored woodlands, and they moved to the tract reluctantly.

Besides resenting the location of the reserves, the Indians believed that they had been cheated in other ways during the transactions in 1851. At Traverse des Sioux, they asserted, the whites had tricked them into signing a "traders' paper" which had never been explained to them. It gave to traders and mixed-bloods for claims against the Indians some $400,000, which would otherwise have been paid to the tribes in cash.

By 1857 land-hungry white settlers had again crowded close to the reservation boundaries, and they began to clamor for a further reduc-

3

tion of the Indians' territory. Thus in the spring of 1858 several Sioux chiefs, tempted by the thought of increased annuity payments, accompanied their agent, Joseph R. Brown, to Washington, D.C., to sign still another pair of treaties. They agreed to give up the strip of land along the north side of the Minnesota River — nearly a million acres — for a price to be fixed by the United States Senate, but it was two years before Congress appropriated thirty cents an acre in payment. After the usual traders' claims had been satisfied, the Lower Sioux received little cash, and the Upper Sioux had coming only about half the original amount voted by the Senate. Such traders' claims soon became a source of bitter complaint among Indians of both bands.

Writing to President Abraham Lincoln on March 6, 1862, over five months before the uprising, Episcopal Bishop Henry B. Whipple, dedicated friend of the Indians, summed up the evils and dangers in the government's Indian policies. The bishop called attention to the frauds in the treaty system and advocated its replacement by a plan that would make the Indians wards of the government. The red men, he said, "cannot live without law. We have broken up, in part, their tribal relations and they must have something in their place." He scored the appointment of Indian agents under a political spoils system. He recommended the abandonment of cash annuities, which flowed directly into the traders' hands, and suggested the government provide instead more goods, seeds, farm implements, and such benefits as schools to make the Native Americans self-supporting.

The treaties of 1851 and 1858 had contained provisions designed to encourage the nomadic Sioux to become farmers. But most of them had remained "blanket Indians," pursuing their old hunting and fishing culture. They derided the farmer Indians, called them "cut-hairs" and

THIS MAP *shows how the "Suland" in southern Minnesota was reduced by the treaties of 1851 and 1858. In 1862 the Sioux were living in the narrow ribbon of reservation along the south side of the upper Minnesota River.* MAP BY ALAN OMINSKY.

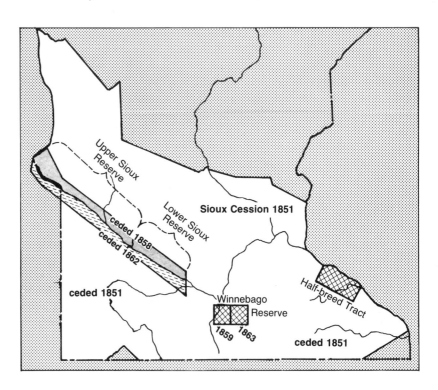

"breeches Indians," and resented what they regarded as the white man's attempt to divide the tribe. In 1861, Brown, who had successfully persuaded over two hundred Sioux to become farmers, was replaced as agent by Thomas J. Galbraith, a political appointee and a newcomer to the frontier.

An incident that further lessened the Sioux's esteem for the white man concerned Inkpaduta (or Scarlet Point), an outlawed Wahpekute chief. In the spring of 1857 he and a small band of renegade Lower Sioux murdered over thirty persons at Lake Okoboji, Iowa, in the so-called "Spirit Lake massacre." Then they departed for Jackson County, Minnesota, where they killed several more persons. Inkpaduta escaped to Dakota Territory and easily eluded the infantry detachments sent to capture him. In desperation, the Indian office at Washington notified the Minnesota Sioux that they would be held responsible for the apprehension of Inkpaduta, and that no annuities would be paid until the culprit was brought in. Chief Little Crow of the Mdewakanton voluntarily led a futile hunt for the renegade, and soon afterward the Indian office withdrew its absurd requirement.

The failure of the Great White Father to punish Inkpaduta's small band of murderers was considered by Dr. Thomas S. Williamson, a veteran missionary to the Sioux, "the primary cause" of the 1862 uprising. Whether Williamson's evaluation is valid or not, the Spirit Lake affair further decreased the Indians' respect for the white man.

In 1862 several other factors heightened the chances of revolt. One of them was the Dakotas' realization that many of the young white "warriors" had left for southern battlefields. Another was a winter of near-starvation in 1861–62 brought on by a crop failure the previous fall. A third was the tardy arrival of the Indians' annuity goods and cash, traditionally received "so soon as the prairie grass was high enough for pasture"—usually about the end of June for the Lower Sioux and two weeks later for the Upper bands. But in 1862 June and July passed, and the money did not arrive. This delay was probably the most important immediate cause of the Sioux Uprising. There were two reasons why the money did not reach the Indians on schedule—one was the tardy action of Congress in appropriating the funds; the other was a month-long discussion in the treasury department over whether to pay the Indians in paper currency instead of scarce gold. It was not until August 16 that $71,000 in the customary gold coin arrived in St. Paul.

In the meantime, on July 14 Agent Galbraith was surprised to find some five thousand Indians assembled at the Upper Agency. All were hungry and demanded to know why they should not be fed from the warehouse full of provisions which belonged to them. Galbraith hesitated to depart from the usual custom of handing out the money and provisions at the same time, but he was forced to compromise and issue some food.

Also on hand for the payment at the Upper Agency was a guard of about a hundred soldiers from two companies of the Fifth Minnesota Regiment under Lieutenant Timothy J. Sheehan. On August 4, some five hundred Sioux, mounted and on foot, surrounded the infantry camp, while other Indians broke into the warehouse and carried out sacks of flour. Sheehan ordered his men to aim a loaded howitzer at the door;

SIOUX TEPEES *were pictured along the Mississippi River in Minnesota Territory shortly before the Indians were forced to occupy reservations on the Minnesota River.* FROM *Harper's New Monthly Magazine,* JULY, 1853.

then he boldly walked between the lines of Indians to confer with Galbraith. He persuaded the agent to issue more pork and flour and arrange a conference with the Sioux leaders the next day. On August 6, Sheehan's superior, Captain John S. Marsh, rode up from Fort Ridgely, a military post on the north bank of the Minnesota River some fifty miles southeast of the Upper Agency. Marsh and others prevailed upon Galbraith to make another payment of annuity goods at once if the Indians would go back to their villages without further trouble and wait until the money came. The situation remained tense during the next three days while the provisions were distributed; then the Indians dispersed and all was quiet.

At the Lower Agency, meanwhile, the Sioux had received some supplies early in June and had returned to their villages to await the annuity payment. Early in August Little Crow obtained the agent's pledge that more provisions would be issued to his people. This promise was not kept, and the chief then demanded that the traders extend further credit. This they refused to do, partly because the powerful "soldiers' lodge," a group of armed Indians having the right to enforce discipline over the tribe, had proposed that no traders' claims were to be allowed at the annuity pay table until their demands were heard in open council. The Indians' anger at the traders' refusal of credit was further inflamed when one of the storekeepers, Andrew J. Myrick, remarked brutally, "If they are hungry, let them eat grass" — a statement widely regarded as another immediate cause of the 1862 uprising.

The Sioux remained suspicious and anxious, but quiet. The days passed, and still the annuity money did not arrive. On August 17, 1862, Little Crow attended services at the Episcopal chapel at the Lower Agency and reportedly shook hands with everybody present. But this was a brief calm before the holocaust. The Indian frontier had become extremely combustible, and four braves would soon light the match.

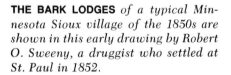

THE BARK LODGES *of a typical Minnesota Sioux village of the 1850s are shown in this early drawing by Robert O. Sweeny, a druggist who settled at St. Paul in 1852.*

2.

ACTON:

AUGUST 17, 1862

THE SIOUX UPRISING in Minnesota was triggered by a trivial egg-finding incident that quickly mushroomed into a major conflict between Indians and whites.

On the bright and beautiful Sunday of August 17, four Indians, who lived some forty miles to the southwest on the Minnesota River, were homeward bound on the Pembina-Henderson trail. They had been hunting in the Big Woods of Kandiyohi and adjacent counties. Around noon they came upon the Robinson Jones homestead in Acton Township, western Meeker County, some three miles southwest of present-day Grove City. They were acquainted with Jones and his wife, who ran a combination post office, lodging place, and store.

In an interview many years later, Chief Big Eagle, a leading participant in the uprising, identified the four Indians as Brown Wing, Breaking Up, Killing Ghost, and Runs Against Something When Crawling—all from Red Middle Voice's Rice Creek encampment of Lower Sioux on the south bank of the Minnesota some distance above the mouth of the Redwood River.

The Indians found some hen's eggs in a nest along Jones's fence. When one of the four took the eggs, another warned him that they belonged to a white man. According to Big Eagle, this made the first Indian angry. He dashed the eggs to the ground and said: "You are a coward. You are afraid of the white man. You are afraid to take even an egg from him, though you are half-starved."

"I am not a coward," the other replied. "I am not afraid of the white man, and to show you that I am not I will go to the house and shoot him. Are you brave enough to go with me?" The other said that he was, and all four went up to the Jones house.

There they reportedly demanded liquor and became angry when Jones refused. In the house at the time were the Joneses' two adopted children—Clara D. Wilson, fifteen years of age, and her infant half brother, who was eighteen months old. Mrs. Jones had gone to visit Howard Baker, her son by a previous marriage, who lived with his wife and two children a half mile to the northeast. Also at the Baker

THE THREE DRAWINGS *on this and the preceding page depict the events of August 17, 1862, in Acton Township, Meeker County, which set off the Sioux Uprising. The picture on page seven shows five Indians approaching the Howard Baker cabin, although there were really only four. Above is the target-shooting contest, and below is the killing of the Baker and Jones families. In it, the artist incorrectly shows the horses hitched to the Websters' wagon. The buildings shown in the sketches were standing in 1883 when John Forgy made these drawings.*

farm were Mr. and Mrs. Viranus Webster, a young couple recently arrived from Wisconsin. They were looking for land in the area and were temporarily living in a covered wagon near the Baker house.

Jones unaccountably left his two children in the store with the Indians and hurried to the Baker place. The Indians followed him there and for a while seemed friendly. They challenged the whites to a target-shooting contest. After firing at a mark fastened to a tree, the Indians reloaded their guns, but the white men neglected to take this precaution.

Suddenly the Indians turned on the settlers and, without warning, fired. Webster, Baker, and Mr. and Mrs. Jones were killed. Mrs. Webster, who stayed in the covered wagon, was not harmed, nor was Mrs. Baker, who fell or jumped into the cellar of the house with a child. The Indians left and, passing the Jones place again, shot and killed Clara Wilson.

Eventually the terrified Mrs. Baker and Mrs. Webster made their way several miles to the home of another settler. From there, word of the murders was sent to Forest City, nearly twenty miles to the east. A party of men hastily set out from Forest City for the Jones house, which they reached late that night. They found the small boy unhurt but hungry. They also found Clara Wilson's body.

The next day, August 18, Judge Abner C. Smith of Meeker County held an inquest. Then the five victims, none of whom had been mutilated, were buried in a single grave in the Ness Norwegian Lutheran Cemetery, a few miles southwest of present-day Litchfield, where a state monument now marks the burial site.

Meanwhile, fully aware that no good would come from having white men's blood on their hands, the four Rice Creek Indians stole several horses and rode pell-mell for their village. The Acton murders apparently had not been planned in advance, as has sometimes been claimed, but they set in motion a series of events that were to have serious consequences for Minnesota and the nation.

THE ACTON MONUMENT *of polished red granite was erected by the state of Minnesota in 1909 on the site of the Baker farm, where the Sioux Uprising began.* PHOTO BY BECKER.

THE MASS GRAVE *of the five settlers killed at Acton is marked by this granite monument in Ness Lutheran Cemetery, southwest of Litchfield. The memorial was dedicated on September 13, 1878.* PHOTO BY BECKER.

9

3.
THE UPRISING BEGINS

MINNESOTA VALLEY BLUFFS *near the Lower Agency are shown as they looked in the 1860s. The villages of the Lower Sioux were all situated within twenty miles of the agency.* FROM *Harper's New Monthly Magazine,* JUNE, 1863.

DARKNESS was approaching on the evening of August 17 when the four killers of the Acton settlers galloped their stolen horses into the Rice Creek village. Their excited stories aroused Red Middle Voice, headman of the village, as well as the other Indians. They felt that the four braves—and possibly the village itself—were in deep trouble. For one thing, white women had been killed, and the Indians believed that this would surely bring the soldiers to punish them and stop the pending annuity payment.

To make matters worse, members of the Rice Creek band were looked down upon by other Lower Sioux because they were trouble-makers and malcontents who had separated from the band of Chief Shakopee (or Little Six). Moreover, the four murderers were regarded as "outsiders" because they were Upper Sioux (Wahpeton) who had married Lower Sioux (Mdewakanton) women. (Two of the four were later killed by their fellow warriors in Dakota Territory.)

Although it was possible that the other Lower Sioux would not support the Rice Creekers and might decide to protect themselves by turning the quartet of miscreants over to the white soldiers, Red Middle Voice and his followers resolved to go to Shakopee's large village (some eight miles downstream near the mouth of the Redwood River) and tell that chief what had happened. Although he later claimed to be, Shakopee was no friend of the whites, and his braves, after hearing the story, said they were eager to make war on the white man. The chief, however, had no intention of committing his people to a general uprising without the backing of other Lower Sioux bands.

Shakopee and Red Middle Voice therefore concluded that a council of chiefs should be convened that very night at Little Crow's village, which was a few miles farther down the Minnesota River near the Lower Agency. Little Crow alone, they felt, had the prestige and ability to lead the Sioux in an all-out war against the whites. The plotters hoped to persuade him to do so, although he had often taken the side of the whites in the past and on occasion wore the white man's

10

dress. Despite the lateness of the hour, riders were sent to summon such leaders as Mankato, Wabasha, Traveling Hail, and Big Eagle to a war council at Little Crow's house, a frame structure built for him by the government.

Dawn was only a few hours away by the time the chiefs and a sizable number of warriors gathered there. Awakened from sleep in a big room on the ground floor, Little Crow sat up to listen to the story of the Acton murders. According to Big Eagle, the chief at first scoffed: "Why do you come to me for advice? Go to the man you elected speaker and let him tell you what to do." (Little Crow was referring bitterly to the fact that Traveling Hail had earlier defeated him for election to the important position of speaker of the Lower Sioux.) As reported by his son, Little Crow then went on to say that he was neither a coward nor a fool. "Braves," he continued, "you are like little children; you know not what you are doing. You are full of the Whiteman's devil water (whisky). You are like dogs in the hot moon, when they run mad and snap at their own shadows. We are only little herds of buffaloes left scattered; the great herds that once covered the prairies are no more. See! The Whitemen are like the locusts, when they fly so thick that the whole sky is a snowstorm. You may kill one, two, ten, yes, as many as the leaves in the forest yonder, and their brothers will not miss them. Kill one, two, ten, and ten times ten will come to kill you. Count your fingers all day long and Whitemen with guns in their hands will come faster than you can count."

The arguments for a general uprising were strong, however, and Little Crow soon agreed to lead the Sioux in a war to drive the settlers from the Minnesota Valley. It has been surmised that he accepted the command to regain his lost prestige as speaker of the Lower Sioux

CHIEF WABASHA (left) was apparently the principal Sioux leader in 1862, but he opposed the war and would not lead the fighting. BIG EAGLE (center) did not favor the war but participated in most of the battles. TRAVELING HAIL (right) also opposed the war and was considered a spokesman for the "cut-hairs." PHOTOS OF WABASHA AND TRAVELING HAIL TAKEN AT NEW YORK CITY IN 1858; BIG EAGLE'S WAS TAKEN IN 1863 OR LATER.

11

ANDREW MYRICK *was a trader hated by the Indians for refusing them credit and remarking, "let them eat grass!" The Sioux killed him and stuffed grass in his mouth.* PHOTO FROM CHIPPEWA COUNTY HISTORICAL SOCIETY.

and to display his military talent—of which he was said to be very vain. Although Wabasha (who may have been the foremost chief), Big Eagle, and some other leaders insisted that it was folly to make war on the whites, they were overruled. Many of the chiefs had little real authority over their bands. Although they and the older men might stand for peace, the young braves could, and did, go counter to their wishes. Once the decision had been made, the chiefs, although reluctant, felt that they had to go along with their people. Big Eagle later reported that the Indians not only decided to wage war on the whites, but also to kill the "cut-hairs," or more civilized Indians, who would not join them in the fight.

Before the council disbanded, Little Crow ordered an attack the following morning on the nearby Lower Agency. "Parties formed and dashed away in the darkness to kill the settlers," said Big Eagle long after. "The women began to run bullets and the men to clean their guns." The fateful decision had been made.

THE SUN rose on August 18 upon another warm summer day at the Lower Agency—a small settlement of traders' stores, quarters for the Indian agent and various government personnel, shops, barns, and other buildings set high on the south bluff overlooking the lush Minnesota River Valley. All was calm, for the residents were not expecting trouble.

Soon after it became light, a large party of painted and armed Sioux braves appeared at the agency. They separated into small groups, surrounding the stores and other principal buildings. At a prearranged signal, bursts of gunfire launched the surprise attack.

The first man to fall dead was James W. Lynd, a former state sena-

JAMES W. LYND, *the first man to be killed at the Lower Agency, had a Sioux wife and two mixed-blood children. He is said to have deserted them a few months before the outbreak for another Indian girl. One historian theorized that his first wife's relatives took revenge.*

GEORGE H. SPENCER *was the only white man taken prisoner at the Lower Agency. Sheltered by an Indian friend, he lived through weeks of captivity and was rescued at Camp Release.* LYND AND SPENCER PHOTOS BY JOEL E. WHITNEY, ST. PAUL, ABOUT 1860 AND 1863.

PHILANDER PRESCOTT, *an aged fur trader and interpreter who had lived peacefully among the Sioux for over forty years, escaped from the Lower Agency only to be killed on the north side of the river.* COPY OF AN UNDATED OIL PAINTING BY AN UNKNOWN ARTIST.

THE SIOUX ATTACKED THE LOWER AGENCY *on August 18. Against a background of burning buildings, the Indians are shown shooting and capturing the whites there. This scene is one of eleven in a circular panorama of the Sioux Outbreak executed about 1893 by three New Ulm artists — Anton Gág, Christian Heller, and Alexander Schwendinger. Painted on a long, continuous roll of canvas, the panorama was set up in a circle around which people walked while viewing it. This one was found in upstate New York by James Taylor Dunn in 1954 and was presented by him to the Minnesota Historical Society.*

THE STONE WAREHOUSE, *built by the government just before the uprising began, is the only original building remaining at the Lower Agency. It has on its gable the initials of Thomas J. Galbraith, the Indian agent in charge there in 1861–62. The building was purchased by the Minnesota Historical Society in 1967.* PHOTO BY KENNETH CARLEY.

tor and an Indian scholar, who was clerking at the store of Nathan and Andrew Myrick, most hated of the traders. Another Myrick employee, George W. Divoll, was also killed when he looked out to see what the commotion was all about. Andrew Myrick managed to escape from the store through a second-story window but was killed before he could reach cover in the brush nearby. Later his corpse was found with grass stuffed in the mouth — the Indians' retaliation for his earlier refusal to grant them credit and his callous challenge, "let them eat grass!"

The surprised whites were easy targets. François La Bathe, another trader, was killed in his store; two clerks were shot at the Louis Robert store; and at the William H. Forbes establishment two men were killed and George H. Spencer was wounded. The latter escaped death with the help of an Indian friend, who has been variously identified as Chaska, His Thunder, and Big Eagle.

A. H. Wagner, superintendent of farms at the agency, and two government employees were killed when they tried to prevent the Indians from taking horses. Little Crow is said to have happened upon the scene as the three men were resisting the thieves. "What are you doing?" Little Crow asked the Indians. "Why don't you shoot these men? What are you waiting for?" The Sioux then fired, killing the two employees and wounding Wagner, who died a little later.

Among those who fled the agency only to be killed on the other side of the river were Dr. Philander P. Humphrey, agency physician, his wife and two children, and Philander Prescott, an elderly fur trader whose wife was Shakopee's mother-in-law. According to Satterlee, the newspaperman who later made an intensive study of white deaths in the uprising, thirteen people were killed in the initial attack on the Lower Agency, and seven more lost their lives in flight. About ten were captured and forty-seven escaped. The last number is rather large because the Indians soon took to plundering and burning buildings, giving the whites a chance to flee across the river on the Redwood Ferry at the foot of the hill below the agency. One of the heroes of the day was undoubtedly the ferryman. Although he could easily have escaped, he stayed at his post, ferried a number of refugees across, and lost his own life. His name, which is not certainly known, has been recorded as Hubert Millier, Charlie Martel, Oliver or Peter Martell, or Jacob Mauley. A small, little-known granite marker, standing amid the brush and trees at the site of Redwood Ferry on the north side of the river, honors the ferryman and gives his name as Charlie Martel.

EXHIBITS *like this, depicting the history of Minnesota's Dakota Indians from about 1750 to the present, are housed in the Lower Sioux Interpretive Center (right), built by the Minnesota Historical Society in 1970. Ongoing archaeological work at the agency has determined that it carried out five basic functions: trading, Indian housing, and religious, central administration, and other government-operated services.* PHOTOS BY CARLEY.

THIS CRUDE SKETCH *of Redwood Ferry was made in June, 1863, by Wilfred J. Whitefield, a member of Henry H. Sibley's expedition to Dakota Territory. It is the only known picture of the ferry that saved so many lives.*

4.

AMBUSH AT REDWOOD FERRY

NEAREST refuge for those who managed to flee from the Lower Agency was Fort Ridgely, some thirteen miles across the river to the east. It wasn't much of a fort, but it was the only military post in southwestern Minnesota.

The fort's garrison on August 18 numbered seventy-six men and two officers of Company B of the Fifth Minnesota Regiment. Most of the soldiers had never seen combat, but their commander, Captain Marsh of Fillmore County, had fought in the Civil War with a Wisconsin regiment at the first battle of Bull Run. Although a bold young officer, he apparently knew little about fighting Indians.

Marsh first learned the startling news of the Indian outbreak about 10:00 A.M. on August 18 from J. C. Dickinson, the boardinghouse operator at the Lower Agency, who had escaped via the ferry with his family. With other frightened refugees, the Dickinsons had made their way to Fort Ridgely in a wagon.

When more fugitives arrived to confirm Dickinson's story, Marsh went into action. First he dispatched Corporal James C. McLean for help. Only the day before, Lieutenant Sheehan had left the post with fifty men of Company C, Fifth Minnesota, bound for Fort Ripley on the Mississippi River. They would still be within reach. Marsh sent Sheehan a message vibrant with urgency: "It is absolutely necessary that you should return with your command immediately to this post. The Indians are raising hell at the Lower Agency."

Leaving nineteen-year-old Lieutenant Thomas P. Gere with twenty-nine men to hold the fort, Marsh started for the Lower Agency with forty-six enlisted men and interpreter Peter Quinn. Marsh and Quinn were mounted on mules; the other men rode most of the way in wagons. On the road the soldiers met numbers of excited settlers, and the Reverend Samuel D. Hinman, Episcopal missionary at the Lower Agency, whose sermon Little Crow had heard the day before. The missionary is said to have warned Marsh that the uprising was serious and that he would be outnumbered if he went as far as Redwood Ferry. Other refugees apparently also cautioned Marsh, but he refused to heed their warnings. At Faribault's Hill, about three miles from

THE REVEREND SAMUEL D. HINMAN, *Episcopal missionary to the Sioux, tried to warn Captain Marsh of the seriousness of the Indian revolt. Only a month before the outbreak, the cornerstone had been laid for Hinman's church at the Lower Agency. It was destroyed during the uprising.*

15

the agency, the soldiers descended from the bluff into the river bottom. They passed houses in flames and saw numerous corpses along the road, including those of the ferryman and Dr. Humphrey and his family.

About a mile from the ferry the men left the wagons and proceeded in single file. At the landing the grass was thick and a heavy growth of hazel and willow brush offered excellent cover along both sides of the river. It was an ideal place for an ambush, and that is exactly what awaited the soldiers. Scores of Indians, with guns ready, lay concealed as the troops pulled up at the ferry shortly after noon.

They found the flat-bottomed ferryboat conveniently moored as if waiting to take them across. The Indians apparently hoped that the soldiers would board the boat and thus present an easy target. Standing across the river in full view of Marsh and his men was a "cut-hair" named White Dog. Through interpreter Quinn, Marsh began to talk with the Indian, who supposedly told the soldiers to come over and hold a council. (Later at his trial White Dog said that he then discovered the ambush and warned Marsh and his men to stay back.)

The soldiers, however, made no move to cross. Then a single shot rang out, and at once Indians sprang up among the trees and bushes and fired. Quinn and at least twelve soldiers fell dead. Marsh's mule was killed under him, but he managed to rally his men for a volley at Indians who had taken over the ferryhouse behind him.

Finding himself cut off on three sides, Marsh led his men along the only possible escape route—a thicket of varying width that extended downstream for about two miles. Here the soldiers were pretty well sheltered from Indian fire. As the afternoon wore on, they made their way along the river to the end of the brush. Once there, they could see the Indians ahead, blocking their path to the fort. Marsh decided the one course of action left was to cross the river and go down the south side. A strong swimmer, he began to lead the soldiers across. He had gone only part of the way when a cramp seized him. He drowned despite efforts to save him.

It was then left to Sergeant John F. Bishop, who was only nineteen years old, to lead fifteen survivors, including five wounded men, back to Fort Ridgely. This he did, successfully reaching the post after nightfall. Eight more infantrymen later returned safely.

Under the circumstances, it was a miracle that any of the soldiers escaped from the ambush. As it was, twenty-four men were lost, including the commander. Only one Indian was reported killed. The skirmish at Redwood Ferry encouraged the Indians, for they found that "They could kill the white men like sheep."

WHILE the morning of August 18 was a nightmare of butchery, looting, and fire at the Lower Agency, all was quiet for a time at Yellow Medicine. The dozen or so buildings there, including a substantial brick structure that served both as a warehouse and the residence of Agent Galbraith, stood on high ground on the west side of the Yellow Medicine River about a mile from its junction with the Minnesota. In the valley below were several traders' stores.

About two weeks earlier, war with the Indians had looked imminent at the Upper Agency. But the Sioux had dispersed after more provisions were given them, and, believing the trouble was over, Sheehan's soldiers had departed. Galbraith also decided to leave. Demonstrating little understanding of the immediate situation, he recruited mixed-bloods and employees at the agency to form a company of Civil War volunteers known as the Renville Rangers. With them he set out for Fort Snelling near St. Paul on August 13. Big Eagle later said that the Sioux "thought the whites must be pretty hard up for men to fight the South, or they would not come so far out on the frontier and take half-breeds or anything to help them."

Rumors of the uprising began reaching the Upper Agency about noon on the eighteenth. Although the whites there at first declined to believe that anything serious was afoot, Dr. J. L. Wakefield, the agency physician, sent his wife and two children toward Fort Ridgely with George H. Gleason, a government employee. Near the Redwood River, Gleason and Mrs. Wakefield encountered two Lower Sioux, Hapa (who was drunk) and Chaska, a farmer Indian. Hapa shot and killed Gleason, but Chaska prevented his companion from harming Mrs. Wakefield and her children. He took them to Shakopee's camp and protected them until they were freed some five weeks later at Camp Release.

In the afternoon, the Wahpeton living near the agency and representatives of some other Upper Sioux bands held a council to decide

5.
WAR COMES TO THE UPPER AGENCY

THIS DUPLEX *for agency employees has been reconstructed by the Minnesota Historical Society in Upper Sioux Agency State Park located southeast of Granite Falls. In the foreground is part of the old agency road.* PHOTO BY CARLEY.

SOME SIOUX INDIANS *and Thomas S. Williamson (third from the left) are shown standing before the missionary's house at Pajutazee.* PHOTO BY WHITNEY, PROBABLY TAKEN JUST BEFORE THE UPRISING IN 1862.

THOMAS S. WILLIAMSON *(left) and* **STEPHEN R. RIGGS** *were veteran missionaries to the Sioux. Williamson, who was a doctor of medicine, established a mission at Lac qui Parle in 1835. He moved to Pajutazee in 1852. Riggs went to the Minnesota country in 1837 to aid Williamson. In 1854 he founded a new mission at Hazelwood, from which he fled in 1862. The two men were friends for over forty years, and both helped translate the Bible into the Dakota language.* ENGRAVING OF WILLIAMSON FROM ALBERT B. MARSHALL, *History of the First Presbyterian Church of Minneapolis* (MINNEAPOLIS, 1910); PHOTO OF RIGGS BY WHITNEY, 1860.

whether to join the Lower Sioux in warring against the whites. A long, heated debate failed to produce a clear-cut decision. Among the staunchest advocates for peace were such Wahpeton Christian leaders as John Other Day (who had a white wife and a mixed-blood child), Chief Akepa, Simon Anawangmani, and Paul Mazakutemani (better known as Little Paul), who was speaker of the Upper Sioux. These men did not favor war, and they warned white friends of the danger before the council was over.

Early that evening the resourceful Other Day herded most of the people at the agency into the brick warehouse. He stood guard during

CHIEF AKEPA *(right) and* **LITTLE PAUL** *or Paul Mazakutemani (oval right) denounced the uprising in Sioux councils. Akepa was widely respected for his knowledge of diseases and remedies, and he ministered to the Sioux prisoners at Mankato during the winter of 1862–63. Little Paul, who had been educated by the missionaries, was speaker of the Upper Sioux. He used his talent for oratory in the Sioux councils to work for peace.* ENGRAVING OF LITTLE PAUL FROM ISAAC V. D. HEARD, *History of the Sioux War* (NEW YORK, 1863); PHOTO OF AKEPA TAKEN IN 1858.

the night, promising to lead the whites to safety in the morning. That night the Indians attacked and burned the trading stores in the valley below, killing one employee and badly wounding two others — Peter Patoile and Stewart B. Garvie. Patoile made a dramatic escape by crawling or walking for thirteen days until he reached a settlement about forty miles north of St. Cloud. Garvie managed to join the group in the warehouse (which several days later was looted and damaged by the Indians, as were most of the agency buildings).

At daybreak on Tuesday, August 19, Other Day led the sixty-two refugees across the Minnesota and onto the prairie on the north side. Many of them were on foot; some (including Garvie) were riding in wagons and buggies. In this party were Dr. Wakefield and the families of Other Day, Galbraith, his assistant Nelson Givens, and others. Three days of dangerous travel under Other Day's skillful guidance brought the group to Cedar City in McLeod County, where Garvie died. The rest went on to Hutchinson, from which point they scattered to such settlements farther east as Glencoe, Carver, Shakopee, and St. Paul.

Near the Minnesota River three miles above the Upper Agency was

JOHN OTHER DAY *fought on the side of the whites during the uprising. In revenge, the Indians burned his home and destroyed his carefully cultivated fields near the Upper Agency. When, after the war, the government awarded him $2,500 for his bravery, Other Day used the money to buy a farm near Henderson.* PHOTO BY WHITNEY, 1862.

ESCAPEES *from the Riggs and Williamson missions near the Upper Agency are pictured resting and eating during their flight on August 21, 1862. Adrian J. Ebell, who was a member of the group, took this photograph. It is the only one known to exist that was taken during the uprising. Riggs is seated directly in front of the woman standing by the wagon wheel.*

THE UPPER SIOUX AGENCY *buildings probably looked like this before they were burned by the Dakota Indians in 1862. The warehouse and agent's quarters are shown at far right.* DRAWING BY CHESTER KOZLAK.

the Pajutazee (meaning "yellow medicine") mission of Dr. and Mrs. Williamson. Two or three miles to the northwest lay the Hazelwood mission of the Reverend Stephen R. Riggs and his wife Mary. On Monday night, friendly Indians informed the Williamsons of the uprising, but the missionaries did not feel they were in personal danger. Antoine Renville, a mission elder, and Little Paul hurried to Hazelwood to warn the Riggs family, but they were equally hard to convince of the seriousness of the situation. After midnight, however, the Hazelwood mission staff took to an island in the Minnesota River for greater safety. Next morning Riggs visited the deserted Upper Agency and decided to flee the area. After his party got under way late Tuesday, it was joined by the family of Jonas Pettijohn, a teacher at Chief Red Iron's village farther upriver, and by several people from the Williamson mission, including Williamson's son-in-law, Andrew Hunter, and Mr. and Mrs. D. Wilson Moore, a New Jersey couple on their honeymoon.

This party of more than thirty people also took the hazardous route along the north side of the river and miraculously escaped harm. It bivouacked in the rain on Wednesday night, and by noon on Friday, August 22, reached Birch Coulee, sixteen miles west of Fort Ridgely. There the Williamsons caught up. They had remained at Pajutazee for twenty-four hours after the others fled. They did not leave until Wednesday, when they learned that Amos W. Huggins, a teacher who had lived among the Wahpeton since childhood, had been killed the day before at Lac qui Parle, thirty miles upriver.

After the group reached Birch Coulee, Hunter went ahead and "crawled into" Fort Ridgely, as Riggs later put it. He found the post already crowded with refugees and learned that it had been attacked during the day. The party would be better advised, he was told, to continue traveling toward the river settlements farther east. The group did so, reaching Henderson on Monday, doubtless more sure than ever that "God Is the Refuge of His Saints," in the words of a hymn the missionaries had taught their Sioux charges.

20

THIS DRAWING *shows what happened to many families during the uprising. The man lies dead, the woman is being taken captive, and the child's fate is not yet known.* FROM *Harper's New Monthly Magazine,* OCTOBER, 1875.

6.

INDIAN RAIDS ALONG THE FRONTIER

DEATH and terror spread quickly throughout the beautiful Minnesota Valley; indeed, panic seized all the settled portions of the state as marauding Indians attacked white settlers in an ever-widening area. Although the principal action of the Sioux Uprising was concentrated in the region bordering the river, events in this major Indian war were to touch more than twenty Minnesota counties before it was over.

Small groups of Sioux fell upon isolated homesteads along the edge of the frontier. Settlers who banded together for strength in flight often offered no resistance and succeeded only in presenting a conveniently concentrated target. In some instances, whole families were wiped out, while in others the men were shot, and the women and children were either killed or taken prisoner. But the Indians' actions were unpredictable, and in a few cases whites who showed fight were allowed to go free. The Sioux looted cabins, took cattle, horses, and oxen, and filled wagons with plunder. They burned barns, haystacks, and some dwellings, although many of the latter were left standing. A federal commission investigating property damage in 1863, however, reported to Congress that not all the devastation could be attributed to the Sioux. It stated that freebooting whites later "completed what the . . . savage had spared."

Seldom has warfare been so one-sided. While hundreds of settlers were killed, very few Indians lost their lives. For one thing, many whites did not have guns and those who did were often too panic-stricken to use them. Moreover, the element of surprise gave the Sioux a tremendous initial advantage. Settlers in Renville and Brown counties—the two areas where loss of life was greatest—were largely Germans. They had lived on friendly terms with the Dakota, whom they knew as wandering, usually hungry, beggars, and at first they could not believe that the Indians were bent on anything as serious as murder.

21

MILFORD STATE MONUMENT *west of New Ulm commemorates the deaths of fifty-two persons killed in the area. The figure symbolizes Memory.* PHOTO BY ROBERT C. WHEELER.

MRS. JOSEPH R. BROWN, *a Sisseton, and her children were captured early in the uprising. Little Crow personally guarded them until they were rescued at Camp Release.* FROM AN EARLY TINTYPE.

A good example of this attitude can be found in the story of thirteen families farming near what is now Sacred Heart. Learning that the Indians were making trouble, these Germans gathered on the evening of August 18 at the home of Paul Kitzman in Flora Township, Renville County, and prepared to flee as a group. Traveling all night in eleven ox-drawn wagons, they had covered about half the distance to Fort Ridgely by sunrise. Soon after, a party of Sioux warriors overtook them. The Indians, at least one of whom Kitzman knew well, assured them that it was the Chippewa who were on the warpath. They persuaded the Germans to return to their homes, promising to escort them safely there. When the settlers reached one of the houses, the Indians suddenly turned on them, killing the men and some of the women and children—twenty-five persons in all. One of the group, Mrs. Justina Krieger, who was wounded and seemed dead, will reappear in the chapter on Birch Coulee.

Milford Township in Brown County, bordering the eastern edge of the Lower Sioux reservation, had the highest death rate of any township in the state. Lying immediately west of New Ulm, it was well populated by German families at the time of the uprising. On August 18, Indians from the Sioux villages nearby swooped down on their unsuspecting neighbors, killing over fifty before nightfall. The victims' names are recorded on the unusual Milford State Monument, which stands six miles west of New Ulm on Brown County Road 29. The loss of life in this township was swelled by the deaths on August 18 of four members of a recruiting party which had left New Ulm in several wagons accompanied by a brass band. The procession was ambushed at a bridge over a ravine five miles west of the town.

The Sioux also attacked a wagon and team driven by Francis Patoile, a Yellow Medicine trader, about ten miles upriver from New Ulm. Accompanying Patoile were one or two other men and three girls — Mary Anderson, Mattie Williams, and Mary E. Schwandt. The men were killed by the attackers; Miss Anderson was severely wounded and died a few days later after being taken captive. The other two girls were also made prisoners and, after having to submit to the unwelcome attentions of Sioux men, were freed at Camp Release. Mary Schwandt, whose narrative describing her captivity and the killing of other members of her family has come down to us, credited a friendly Indian woman, Snana, with protecting her. A state monument in Renville County commemorates the deaths of six other members of the Johann Schwandt family.

Mary Schwandt's story is only one of many reminiscences that have found their way into print. Some of these deal with the experiences of women captives; others describe in grim detail the terrible ordeals suffered by refugees who miraculously escaped death. Such recollections comprise a body of literature commonly characterized as "atrocity" stories of the Sioux War. The lurid reports made by many terrified survivors in most cases have not been confirmed, although some atrocities undoubtedly were committed. Serious scholars, however, feel that the number is far smaller than was believed at the time of the uprising.

One of the most interesting tales of Indian captivity concerns the wife and thirteen children of Joseph R. Brown, the former Sioux agent who lived in an elegant stone house on the north side of the Minnesota about seven miles below the Upper Agency. Brown was absent from

home when, early on the morning of August 19, his Dakota wife led some twenty-six persons toward Fort Ridgely. They had traveled only six miles when Cut Nose and other Indian desperadoes stopped them and demanded that the whites be killed. Mrs. Brown bravely stood up in the wagon, reminding the Indians in their own language that she was a Sisseton and that the wrath of her Upper Sioux relatives would be brought down on the heads of the attackers if they committed murder. Impressed, the Indians reluctantly let the men in the Brown party escape, then took the women and children to Little Crow's house. Samuel J. Brown, a son, later described the experience: "When mother entered, the chief arose from his couch . . . and greeted her very cordially, and then handed her a cup of cold water. . . . We were all hurried upstairs and told to remain quiet. The chief gave us robes and blankets." Eager to keep the Upper Sioux sympathetic to his cause, Little Crow personally watched out for Mrs. Brown and her children until they were freed at Camp Release. The ruins of the Brown house are now preserved in a state park.

As the uprising gathered momentum, the Indians spread out to strike more remote areas on the fringes of settlement. Along the boundary between Swift and Kandiyohi counties, at least forty miles north of the Upper Agency, the Sioux on August 20 killed fourteen or more whites in the Scandinavian settlement of West Lake. There the families of Anders P. and Daniel P. Broberg were virtually wiped out after attending religious services at the home of Andreas L. Lundborg, a neighbor. The scene of this attack is preserved in Monson Lake State Park, and a state monument marks the graves of these Swedish settlers in Lebanon Cemetery near New London.

Many individual acts of heroism, both Indian and white, are woven into the fabric of the Sioux Uprising. Among them is the story of Guri Endreson, who lived with her husband Lars and their five children near Willmar in Kandiyohi County. On August 21, Indians attacked the Endreson homestead, killing Lars and one son and badly wounding the other boy. Guri and her youngest daughter escaped harm by hiding in the cellar. After the Indians left, taking the two older girls with them, Guri and her two remaining children set out for Forest City, the nearest settlement, which was some thirty miles away. Stopping at a cabin, she found two severely wounded men, whom she managed to help into a wagon. Then she drove the entire party to safety. Her two

23

older daughters escaped from their Indian captors and joined their mother at Forest City. A state monument erected in 1907 marks her grave in Vikor Lutheran Church Cemetery north of Willmar.

On the western border of the state near present-day Ortonville, the Sioux on August 21 killed several traders' clerks and government employees at or near a trading post there. About forty miles south of the Upper Agency near Lake Shetek in Murray County, the Indians on August 20 attacked an advance settlement of some eleven families. Betrayed by an Indian named Pawn, the Lake Shetek settlers left their refuge in a sturdy cabin and sought shelter in a swamp that became known as "Slaughter Slough." There the Indians killed at least fifteen of them, and a settler, Thomas Ireland, claimed to have shot Chief Lean Bear. Ireland, Mrs. Lavina Eastlick (who was badly wounded), William J. Duley, and Mrs. Alomina Hurd were among the survivors who escaped to tell the grisly Lake Shetek story. Two women settlers at Shetek — Mrs. Julia Wright and Mrs. Laura Duley, wife of William — were captured along with six children by Chief White Lodge's band of Sisseton and forced to roam the Dakota plains for weeks with the Indians. The eight captives were ransomed on the Missouri River in November and reunited with their families.

These are only a few of the many dramatic Indian raids that occurred in an area bisected roughly by a line from Fort Abercrombie, on the Dakota border, southeastward to New Ulm. Inhabitants of twenty-three counties in a region about two hundred miles long by fifty or more miles wide fled eastward, leaving a vast stretch of southern Minnesota completely depopulated. The settlers' panic was increased by the fear that the Winnebago Indians, living on a reservation ten miles south of Mankato, and the Chippewa, in the northern part of the state, would join the Sioux in their attempt to drive the white man from the area. Fleeing refugees temporarily swelled the populations of St. Paul, St. Anthony, Minneapolis, Hastings, St. Cloud, Winona, and other cities in eastern Minnesota. Uneasiness about the uprising spread even to Wisconsin and other states. Many citizens left Minnesota never to return. Others, however, made do with the nearest havens — Fort Ridgely and New Ulm.

PANIC-STRICKEN, *often defenseless settlers, like those shown fleeing from their homes in the Minnesota Valley, were often the victims of Indian attacks during the first days of the uprising.* SCENE FROM GÁG-HELLER-SCHWENDINGER PANORAMA.

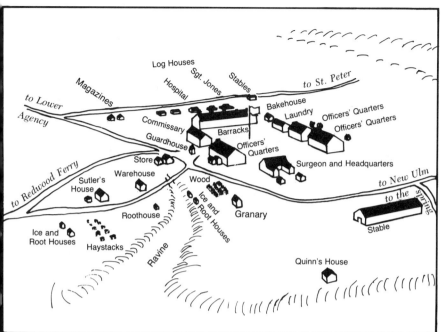

PLAN *of Fort Ridgely, 1862.* DRAWING BY ALAN OMINSKY.

7.

ATTACKS ON FORT RIDGELY

THROUGHOUT the day and into the night of August 18, refugees thronged into Fort Ridgely. By sundown the place bulged with more than two hundred fugitives, a majority of them women and children. Many were greatly upset and enough were wounded to tax the post's limited hospital capacity.

Although the frightened settlers were relieved to reach the fort in safety, some must have had misgivings about their haven's obvious weaknesses. Probably named for Captain Randolph Ridgely, an artillery hero who died in the Mexican War, Fort Ridgely was a United States Army post established in 1853 in the northwest corner of Nicollet County so that troops could keep an eye on the Sioux. Neither in location nor construction was it well suited to repulse attack. It sat on a spur of high prairie tableland 150 feet above the valley floor. Deep ravines to the east, north, and southwest offered attackers easy avenues of approach to within musket range. The open prairie extended to the northwest.

The fort itself, as well as the terrain, presented problems to defenders. Completely devoid of a stockade, the post was merely a collection of detached and unfortified buildings. The chief ones, grouped around a parade ground ninety yards wide, included a large two-story stone barracks on the north side, a one-story commissary at the northwest corner, two-story frame buildings serving as officers' quarters on the east and west sides, and the commandant's and surgeon's quarters on the southwest corner. Behind the barracks to the north stood a row of log houses for civilian employees and a small log hospital. Stables for the horses lay across the New Ulm road to the south. Ammunition magazines stood out on the prairie two hundred yards northwest of the fort. To the west near the road to Redwood Ferry were the sutler's house and other outbuildings.

LIEUTENANT THOMAS P. GERE *had been in the army only eight months when he was left in charge of Fort Ridgely. The youthful commander had the mumps during the first attack on the fort.* PHOTO BY WHITNEY, 1860s.

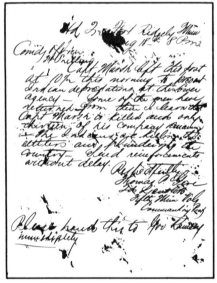

GERE'S *hurried message to Governor Ramsey was ink-stained but reasonably legible.*

LIEUTENANT TIMOTHY J. SHEEHAN, *an Irishman from Albert Lea, was twenty-six years of age when he took over command of Fort Ridgely from Gere on August 19.* PHOTO BY WHITNEY, 1860s.

It will be recalled that Fort Ridgely was left in charge of a boy commander, Lieutenant Gere, when Captain Marsh and his men departed Monday forenoon for Redwood Ferry and disaster. Gere himself was ill, and he had only twenty-two soldiers available for active duty (the rest were sick or on hospital detail). Also on hand and very helpful were Dr. Alfred Müller, the post surgeon, Benjamin H. Randall, the sutler, and Ordnance Sergeant John Jones.

For some reason no well was ever dug at the fort. Sutler Randall saw to it that tubs, barrels, and all other available containers were filled with water from the spring below the river bluff. Dr. Müller cared for wounded refugees as they arrived. When they filled the little hospital, he had cots set up in his quarters, where Mrs. Müller took charge. Several women refugees helped by acting as nurses, making bandages, or preparing meals.

About noon a stagecoach pulled up at the fort and out climbed four guards and Cyrus G. Wyckoff, a clerk representing Clark W. Thompson, superintendent of Indian affairs in St. Paul. Ironically, they brought the Sioux annuity money—$71,000 in gold—the earlier arrival of which might have prevented the uprising. Now only an added burden to Gere, the kegs of money were hidden in one of the buildings and eventually returned to St. Paul.

As the hours passed and more and more refugees arrived with wild tales, Gere became increasingly anxious for word of Marsh's expedition. Finally, after dark, the first two survivors of the Redwood Ferry ambush reached the fort with the dire news of the death of Marsh and twenty-three men. Gere immediately wrote a hurried dispatch to the commanding officer at Fort Snelling and to Governor Alexander Ramsey.

Gere's ink-splattered, hastily written message dated at 8:00 P.M. on August 18 is preserved in the Minnesota State Archives. It reads: "Capt[.] Marsh left this post at 10½ this morning to prevent Indian depredations at the Lower Agency. Some of the men have returned— from them I learn that Capt[.] Marsh is killed and only thirteen of his company remaining. The Indians are killing the settlers and plundering the country. Send reinforcements without delay." In an afterthought, Gere scribbled at the bottom, "Please hand this to Gov[.] Ramsey immediately [.]"

Private William J. Sturgis set out in the darkness to carry Gere's message the 125 miles or so to Fort Snelling. Using several horses and traveling part of the time by wagon, he made the trip in eighteen hours. On the way, Sturgis stopped at St. Peter, where he found the Renville Rangers recruited by Galbraith and Lieutenant Norman K. Culver of the Fifth Minnesota who had accompanied them. He asked these men to go at once to the fort.

After midnight Gere wrote again to Sheehan, who after receiving Marsh's earlier message was heading back with his men to Ridgely from the northeast. Said Gere to Sheehan: "Force your march returning. Captain Marsh and most of his command were killed yesterday at the Lower Agency. Little Crow and about 600 Sioux warriors are now approaching the fort and will undoubtedly attack us. About 250 refugees have arrived here for protection. The Indians are killing men, women, and children."

26

Actually, while Gere wrote, the Indians were celebrating their triumphs and were not yet ready to attack the fort. Had they stormed it that night or on Tuesday morning, almost certainly they could have taken Fort Ridgely and thereby opened a clear route to the Mississippi. But for all Gere and his small force knew, the Indians would be upon them at any moment, and they took what precautions they could. The women and children were crowded into the stone barracks and pickets were posted around the fort. Some of these were civilians who had been given muskets from the post's small supply. Everyone was on the alert, but the night passed quietly.

At about nine o'clock the next morning (August 19), Indians on horseback, in wagons, and on foot began congregating on the prairie west of the fort. Little Crow, as well as Mankato and Big Eagle, recognized that Ridgely should be assaulted at once, and in this early morning council they tried to convince the others of that fact. But they were overruled by the young braves, who preferred to attack New Ulm, where there were stores to loot and pretty girls to capture. As the post's lookouts watched through a telescope, the gathering broke up, and the Indians moved off across the river toward New Ulm.

The young braves' decision undoubtedly saved Fort Ridgely, for it permitted reinforcements to arrive. During the morning the post welcomed Sheehan and his men, who had marched all night after Marsh's messenger found them encamped near Glencoe, forty-two miles away. Lieutenant Sheehan took over command of the fort from the ailing Gere. Toward evening the Renville Rangers arrived with Galbraith and Culver after a march from St. Peter. Sheehan now had about 180 "effectives" with which to defend the fort. These consisted

THE SECOND BATTLE of Fort Ridgely is depicted in this artist's conception. In the background and at lower left are ravines that offered attackers handy cover. The burning buildings, set ablaze by well-placed cannon fire, are the stable (foreground) and the sutler's store (left center). DRAWING BY PAUL WALLER.

SERGEANT JAMES G. McGREW, *an able artillerist stationed at the northeast corner of the fort, manned one of the howitzers that kept the Sioux from capturing Fort Ridgely.*

of fifty-two men of Company B, fifty men of Company C, fifty Renville Rangers, and about twenty-five armed citizens under Sutler Randall, as well as Dr. Müller, one or two others — and Sergeant Jones.

As later events were to indicate, Jones may well have been the most important of the lot. Fortunately, Ridgely had been an artillery post and Jones, who was an ordnance expert, was in charge of the munition stores and cannon that had been left at the fort the previous year when United States troops were temporarily withdrawn. He had taught the men of Company B to load and fire these pieces, and now he formed three gun detachments. Jones and another experienced artilleryman named Dennis O'Shea handled a six-pound fieldpiece placed at the southwest corner. Two twelve-pound mountain howitzers were manned by Sergeant James G. McGrew, an able artillerist of Company B, and by J. C. Whipple, a refugee from the Lower Agency who had gained experience in the use of mounted firearms during the Mexican War. Thus prepared, the garrison awaited attack.

It came early in the afternoon of August 20, when Little Crow was able to collect perhaps four hundred warriors (but probably less than that) after the Sioux had been repulsed at New Ulm the day before. Some of the Indians—Little Crow is said to have been one of them—made a distracting demonstration on the west side of the fort, while the main body of the Sioux crept up the east ravine and struck at the northeast corner, gaining some of the outbuildings.

Sheehan at first formed his men on the parade ground, but after one soldier was killed and another wounded he told them to take cover and fire at will, especially in support of the cannon. Whipple stationed his howitzer near the northeast point of the parade ground. McGrew wheeled his gun to the northwest corner, and, running the howitzer out amidst a shower of bullets, aimed it toward the northeast. The converging fire of the two guns, aided by a heavy discharge of muskets from supporting troops, drove the Indians away from the buildings and back into the ravine. Meanwhile Sergeant Jones and his

SERGEANT JOHN JONES *and his artillerymen kept the Sioux from overwhelming the small garrison at Fort Ridgely. A large measure of responsibility for the safety of the fort and its many refugees fell to Jones while Gere had the mumps. During the first attack, his wife gave birth to a stillborn child.* PHOTO TAKEN IN THE 1860s.

cannon, in a particularly exposed position, warded off other Indian attackers on the south and west. After their first rush failed, the Sioux continued firing from a distance for about five hours. During that time, Sheehan decided to rescue the supplies from the magazines on the exposed prairie. The men detailed for that mission were safely covered by McGrew's gun while they brought the ammunition into the stone buildings.

After nightfall the Indians withdrew to the Lower Agency. The Sioux had never before encountered artillery, and it surprised and disturbed them. One witness reported that the Indians were "mortally afraid" of the "rotten balls," as they called the howitzer shells, which flew into pieces when fired. Heavy rain fell during the night and most of the following day. The defenders of the fort used this time to get more drinking water and to put up barricades of grain sacks and cordwood. A twelve-pound Napoleon gun was moved to the southeast corner under the charge of Sergeant John Bishop.

Not until the afternoon of the next day, Friday, August 22, did the Indians return in much larger force for a "grand affair," as Big Eagle later called it. This time an estimated eight hundred warriors, including some Wahpeton and Sisseton, launched a strong attack led by Little Crow. To conceal their movements until they crept close enough to fire, the Sioux camouflaged their headbands with prairie grass and flowers. They tried to set fire to the roofs with blazing arrows, but the recent rain made this effort largely futile. In a few places where fires did start, the defenders were ready with water.

The attackers' first onslaught was unsuccessful. The next step in their strategy apparently was to wear down the whites with constant fire, then launch an assault from the southwest and defeat the badly outnumbered defenders in hand-to-hand combat. When some Indians gained the stables to the south, well-placed artillery shells set that building afire. The same thing happened to the sutler's house when the Sioux tried to use it for cover.

THIS PAINTING *shows how the attacking Sioux used the trees and ravines near the fort for cover. One of the howitzer shells, which so disturbed the Indians, is shown exploding among them.* SCENE FROM GÁG-HELLER-SCHWENDINGER PANORAMA.

29

MRS. ELIZA MÜLLER, *wife of the post surgeon, bolstered morale by caring for the wounded and aiding the fort's defenders.*

THE STONE COMMISSARY *has been restored and now houses the Fort Ridgely Interpretive Center, completed in 1975 by the Minnesota Historical Society. The foundations of other buildings are marked. The center's exhibits (lower right) are organized around key years and events in the fort's history.* PHOTOS BY CARLEY (BELOW) AND STEVEN PLATTNER (RIGHT).

After hours of shelling and of "demoniac yells," as Gere called them, the Indians appeared set for an all-out attack on the southwest angle through the ravine near it. Mankato is said to have been the leader of this attempt, as Little Crow had been wounded. Just as the Indians were ready to attack, Sergeant Jones and O'Shea double-charged their gun with canister shot, fired accurately, and sent the warriors fleeing in disorder. Other artillery fire by McGrew from a twenty-four pounder that had been set up at the west sally port helped put an end to proceedings. The gallant defenders of Ridgely had won a great victory, and their artillerymen under Jones could take the deepest bows. But no one had been idle. Even noncombatants had assisted by making cartridges from opened spherical case shot when musket ammunition ran low.

Mrs. Eliza Müller, in particular, calmly and efficiently organized the women to produce cartridges in a ground-floor room of the barracks. She also joined the actual fighting at one stage by helping Sergeant Jones wheel a cannon to a spot from which it could be fired at the stables. Constantly busy, she made coffee and carried it to the guards and, with her husband, spent many hours tending the sick and injured. One historian called her the "Clara Barton of the Minnesota frontier." After her death in 1876 she was buried in the Fort Ridgely cemetery, where her gravestone may still be seen.

The defense of Fort Ridgely cost the whites three dead and thirteen wounded. Although the Sioux casualties have been estimated at a hundred, they probably were not that high. Years after, Indians could recall the names of only two dead warriors—Iron Nest and Striped Wing Feathers.

Ridgely's embattled soldiers and citizens, fearing new attacks, suffered through four more anxious days before relief arrived. As soon as he learned of the uprising on August 19, Governor Ramsey gave Henry

H. Sibley, his long-time friend and political rival, a colonel's commission and asked him to head an expedition to put down the outbreak. Although he had no previous military experience, Sibley knew the Dakota — their country, language, and customs — for he had traded among them since his arrival in the Minnesota area twenty-eight years before as the American Fur Company's representative at Mendota. Moving cautiously, the new colonel started the following day for St. Peter with a small force of four companies of the hastily formed Sixth Minnesota Regiment. At St. Peter he met his old hunting friend Jack Frazer, a mixed-blood, who got through from Ridgely with a pessimistic message sent by Sheehan during the lull between the attacks on the fort. Frazer's dark picture of the seriousness of the uprising increased Sibley's caution. He waited at St. Peter for supplies and reinforcements.

At last on August 26 he advanced with 1,400 soldiers. A vanguard of mounted men under Colonel Samuel McPhail went ahead and, to the great joy of Ridgely's defenders, lifted the fort's siege on Wednesday, August 27. (Captain Anson Northup and 175 men from Minneapolis sometimes are credited with being the first of this group to reach the fort.) Sibley's entire force arrived the next day. On August 29 many of the refugees, some of whom had been shut up in the post for eleven days, were removed to St. Paul in the wagons that had brought supplies for Sibley's troops.

Chief Big Eagle, who fought the whites at Fort Ridgely, aptly summed up the importance of the Indian repulse there when he said: "We thought the fort was the door to the valley as far as to St. Paul, and that if we got through the door nothing could stop us this side of the Mississippi. But the defenders of the Fort were very brave and kept the door shut."

COLONEL HENRY H. SIBLEY *commanded the heterogeneous volunteers who put down the Sioux Uprising. A well-known fur trader, he served as Minnesota Territory's first delegate to Congress and as the state's first governor.* ENGRAVING FROM W. H. C. FOLSOM, *Fifty Years in the Northwest* (ST. PAUL, 1888).

8.

THE TWO
BATTLES OF
NEW ULM

THIS UNUSUAL PAINTING *on a barrelhead shows the first battle of New Ulm on August 19. The barricades depicted were on Third Street.* OIL BY GÁG, 1902. BROWN COUNTY HISTORICAL SOCIETY.

WHILE defenders of Fort Ridgely "shut the door" north of the Minnesota River, those of New Ulm effectively halted the Sioux on the south side. Like the fort, the town beat back two Indian assaults— the first one relatively light and the second, a few days later, much heavier.

In 1862 New Ulm was by far the largest settlement near the Sioux reservation. As such it tempted the young braves who were eager to collect the booty it promised. Situated near the junction of the Cottonwood and Minnesota rivers, the town was founded in 1854–55 by members of German colonization societies from Chicago and Cincinnati. Its population in 1860 was 635, and by the time of the Sioux Uprising it probably had close to 900 people.

New Ulm presented an attractive target to the Indians in other ways. They knew that some of the town's young men had gone south to serve in the Union army. They were also aware that the people possessed few guns and little ammunition. Moreover, it was evident to the Sioux that the terrain on which the town stands would make defense difficult. The land rises some two hundred feet in two giant steps from the Minnesota River to the top of a high bluff behind the town. In 1862 most of the houses were spread out along the lower terrace, with an occasional one situated up on the second terrace. These wide steps provided the Sioux with sloping springboards for invasion. To make matters worse for the Germans, woods running along the crest of the bluff behind the town and a slough extending the length of the settlement between the second terrace and the bluff offered the attackers ample cover.

The morning of August 18 was a festive occasion in New Ulm. The people turned out to give a rousing send-off to a recruiting party, heading west over the prairie to enlist Civil War volunteers among the farmers working in the August sunshine. As we have seen, this group was ambushed in Milford Township. The survivors raced back to New Ulm, bringing what was probably the town's first word of the Indian outbreak. About the same time, farm families began to stream into the settlement with the terrifying news.

Great excitement, even panic, seized many of the townspeople, but some defense measures came out of the confusion. Brown County Sheriff Charles Roos and Jacob Nix, a citizen with military experience, organized the men with guns — numbering only about forty — into militia units. Others were armed with pitchforks and similar crude weapons and put to work erecting barricades around approximately three blocks on Minnesota Street from Center to Third North, where there were brick buildings that could be defended.

Many women and children were packed into the town's leading hotel, the Dacotah House, the Erd Building, and other nearby structures. Gottlieb C. Oswald, a thirteen-year-old farm lad at the time, afterward recalled that the Dacotah House got so crowded upstairs that "the women had to go downstairs, discard their hoop skirts and pile them in the back yard. . . . We laughed in spite of our danger."

NEW ULM *as it looked in 1860, showing the terraced terrain on which the town is built along the Minnesota River. Note how the houses were spread out.*

Couriers were dispatched to seek help from St. Peter and neighboring settlements. Sheriff Roos and others led relief parties into the surrounding countryside to bring in farmers who might be hiding or who were unaware of their danger. Monday passed, and that night the townspeople slept uneasily.

Before dawn on August 19, Henry Behnke, a messenger from New Ulm, galloped into St. Peter and awakened William B. Dodd, one of the town's founders. By 4:00 A.M. Dodd was sending men to gather volunteers in other communities. Meanwhile, Behnke rode on to Traverse des Sioux, a mile north of St. Peter, to arouse Charles E. Flandrau, the Minnesota Valley's best-known citizen at the time. A unique figure in the annals of the area, Flandrau had been a conspicuous member of Minnesota's constitutional convention and an Indian agent. In 1857 he had been appointed to the Minnesota Supreme Court. It was natural that New Ulmers should turn to him for help; as an attorney he had accompanied the German claimants to the land office at Winona in 1856 to help them file their first claims for the New Ulm townsite. The genial judge now hastened to St. Peter, where he found Dodd with over a hundred volunteers.

While the main body of the citizen-soldiers at St. Peter was gathering up arms, ammunition, and other necessities for the march to New Ulm, Henry A. Swift, a future state governor, and William G. Hayden, Nicollet County auditor, left by buggy for the town. Also a party of sixteen mounted men set out under the leadership of L. M. Boardman, former Nicollet County sheriff. Swift and Hayden appear to have reached New Ulm around 1:00 P.M., about the same time another squad pulled in from Swan Lake and Nicollet across the river. Boardman's group (which included Horace Austin, another future Minnesota governor) arrived several hours later.

Throughout Tuesday morning the people of New Ulm had worked to strengthen the town's defenses, and refugees had continued to pour in to swell its population. Sixteen men set out on a combination scouting and rescue mission to the farms along the Cottonwood River,

southwest of New Ulm. As the members of this party straggled back toward evening, they were ambushed near the outskirts of New Ulm. Eleven men were killed. One of the group, Luther C. Ives, made a wild ride in a wagon past the Indians and got through.

The first Sioux assault on New Ulm came about 3:00 P.M. on Tuesday, August 19, when perhaps a hundred warriors dismounted on the bluff behind the town and began firing. The small number of citizens with rifles returned the fire as best they could and kept the Indians pretty well at bay. Several men led by Daniel G. Shillock made a sally to a house outside the barricades and helped drive the Sioux back. Some houses were burned at the upriver end of town.

Late in the afternoon the defenders got a big assist from a thunderstorm that seemed to discourage the Indians. Also of considerable help was the fact that the Sioux lacked a leader, for apparently no chiefs were present. The Indians appeared about ready to leave when Boardman and his men arrived from St. Peter in time to get in on the very last of the fighting and to occasion arguments from that day to this over who saved the town on August 19.

Thus ended the first battle of New Ulm. The first person killed was a thirteen-year-old girl named Emilie Pauli, who tried to cross the main street while the fighting was in progress. Five others lost their lives, and at least five persons were wounded.

Flandrau reached New Ulm about ten o'clock that night at the head of a column of some 125 Frontier Guards from St. Peter and Le Sueur. With them came Drs. Asa W. Daniels of St. Peter and Otis Ayer and William W. Mayo of Le Sueur. The latter was the father of the famous brothers, William J. and Charles H. Mayo, who later made Rochester a world-renowned medical center. Dr. Mayo and Dr. William R. McMahan of Mankato set up a hospital in a front room of the Dacotah House, and Drs. Ayer and Daniels did the same in the basement of a store across the street. The presence of so many medical men to help New Ulm's Dr. Carl Weschcke was indeed fortunate.

In addition to taking care of the wounded, Flandrau's forces posted guards around the town and began at once to strengthen its defenses. The men gathered barrels, wagons, and other materials to fortify the street barricades and improve the makeshift barriers between the buildings in the town's hard core area of defense. Next day, August 20, the officers of the various companies of civilian defenders then in New Ulm elected Flandrau their commander and gave him the honorary title of colonel. Dodd was elected second in command, and Salmon A. Buell of St. Peter was named "provost marshal, chief of staff and general manager."

During the week Flandrau's command was enlarged by the arrival of a hundred men from Mankato under Captain William Bierbauer, and two companies of Le Sueur Tigers under Captains William Dellaughter and Edwin C. Sanders. Other units to join Flandrau included Captain Louis Buggert's company of Brown County militia, Captain Aaron M. Bean's Nicollet County Guards, Lieutenant William Huey's St. Peter Guards, Captain Fidel Diepolder's company from Lafayette, and Captain John Bellm's New Ulm militia.

The largest number of citizen-soldiers Flandrau had at one time was about three hundred, most of whom were poorly armed. His defensive strength was weakened when the members of a company from South Bend returned to their Blue Earth County homes after the men heard that the Winnebago were threatening to make trouble there.

In the days following the attack, tension mounted, especially among the more than a thousand women, children, and men without guns crowded into the small barricaded area of New Ulm's main street. Many were forced to remain in the cramped basement quarters of the Erd Building, as a modern plaque to be seen on this greatly remodeled structure points out.

On Saturday morning, August 23, Flandrau's lookouts spotted smoke in the direction of Fort Ridgely. The fires were evidently set by the Sioux to give the impression that the fort had fallen and that the Indians were about to attack New Ulm from the north side of the river.

SIOUX WARRIORS *are shown firing on the town during the second battle of New Ulm on August 23. In the left foreground is an "Indian on a white horse" who was observed and remembered by many defenders. Some identified him as Wabasha.* OIL BY SCHWENDINGER, 1891. BROWN COUNTY HISTORICAL SOCIETY.

Flandrau fell for the ruse to the extent of sending Huey across with seventy-five men. He was cut off by the Sioux, had to retreat toward St. Peter, and did not get back to New Ulm until the next day. The temporary loss of Huey's detachment reduced Flandrau's fighting force to 225 guns or less just as the Indians were ready to attack. This time the Sioux had about 650 braves under such chiefs as Mankato, Wabasha, and Big Eagle. (Little Crow was still out of action from his wound at Ridgely.)

At about 9:30 A.M. the Indians streamed out of the woods onto the prairie west of New Ulm and formed a long, curved line on the upper terrace. Flandrau directed Dodd to meet the Indians well outside the barricades. Describing the attack that followed, Flandrau later wrote: "Their advance upon the sloping prairie in the bright sunlight was a very fine spectacle, and to such inexperienced soldiers as we all were, intensely exciting. When within about one mile and a half of us the mass began to expand like a fan, and increase in the velocity of its approach, and continued this movement until within about double rifle-shot, when it had covered our entire front. Then the savages uttered a terrific yell and came down upon us like the wind."

The yell "unsettled the men a little" and they broke for the rear, passing houses that the advancing Indians immediately occupied. Flandrau's men rallied, however, and regained some of the buildings. "The firing from both sides then became general, sharp and rapid," said Flandrau, "and it got to be a regular Indian skirmish, in which every man did his own work after his own fashion."

About twenty members of the Le Sueur Tigers occupied a large wooden windmill three blocks west of the business district. Their sharp sniping did much to keep the Indians from storming the barricades there. Other men made an effective outpost of the post office in the brick Forster Building, a block west of Minnesota Street.

THE KIESLING HOUSE, *restored in 1973 as the focal point of a small park, is now the only building in downtown New Ulm that looks much as it did during the Sioux attacks. Frederick W. Kiesling, a blacksmith and farrier, built the little house in June, 1861, at 220 North Minnesota Street. Although one of the few structures to escape burning in 1862, it was said to have been filled with hay and ready for the torch in case it had to be abandoned.* PHOTO BY CARLEY.

WILLIAM B. DODD *(on horseback), second in command of the volunteers at New Ulm, was killed by the Sioux while leading citizen-soldiers beyond the south barricade on August 23.* SCENE FROM GÁG-HELLER-SCHWEN-DINGER PANORAMA.

THE NEW ULM STATE MONUMENT *on Center Street was designed by Anton Gág. Dedicated in 1891 to the "Guardians of the Frontier," it has battle scenes in relief, a medallion of Flandrau, and suitable inscriptions.* PHOTO BY BECKER.

Because of their superior numbers, however, the attackers gradually enveloped the town. They might have closed in even faster had not many buildings been burned, leaving an open space they did not care to advance across. Because the wind was from the lower part of the town, the Indians concentrated near the river, where they set fire to buildings and advanced behind the smoke. Flandrau was aware that an attack was taking form on the "wind" side, and about 3:00 P.M. he rallied his men to face a charge of some sixty warriors "on ponies and afoot." This time Flandrau's inexperienced soldiers did not panic but launched a countercharge. Yelling like savages and aided by a volley from the barricades, the white defenders routed the Sioux. Although some fighting continued until dark, Flandrau felt that this charge was the turning point of the battle, for it gave his untrained volunteers increased confidence.

Earlier, Captain Dodd, thinking some riders coming into the lower town were Huey and his men, dashed down the street on his horse to meet the approaching party. As he rode beyond the southern barricade, both he and his horse were shot by Indians in hiding. Dodd got back to his men but died a few hours later.

After nightfall Flandrau ordered that the forty or so buildings still standing outside the barriers be burned. In all, 190 structures in New Ulm were destroyed. Those left were within the barricades, except for the post office, which had been loopholed and commanded much of the front toward the second terrace.

The Indians reappeared on Sunday morning, August 24, fired some harmless long-range shots, attempted to drive off some cattle, and then withdrew. Later that day Flandrau held a council with his officers, and it was decided that New Ulm should be evacuated. Not only was there a critical shortage of ammunition and food, but epidemics of disease threatened the noncombatants who had been huddled for five days "in cellars and close rooms like sheep in a cattle car," as Flandrau put it.

Thus the following morning, after many citizens had given up cherished possessions they wished to take with them, 153 wagons loaded with women, children, sick, and wounded, plus a large number of refugees on foot, began an exodus from New Ulm. They were headed for Mankato, about thirty miles to the east. "A more heart-rending procession was never witnessed in America," declared Flandrau. "It was a melancholy spectacle to see 2,000 people, who a few days before had been prosperous and happy, reduced to utter beggary, starting on a journey . . . through a hostile country, every inch of which we expected to be called upon to defend from an attack." Although the commander accompanied the train, its troop escort was under the immediate charge of Captain E. St. Julien Cox, who had reached New Ulm the day before with 150 well-armed men from Nicollet and Sibley counties. Flandrau considered the journey a dangerous expedient, but the procession reached Mankato safely that night. "Under Providence," he reported, "we got through."

The defenders of New Ulm lost thirty-four dead and sixty wounded. How many Indians were killed is not known. Summarizing the fighting at New Ulm, William W. Folwell, one of the state's leading historians, wrote: "This was no sham battle, no trivial affair, but an heroic defense of a beleaguered town against a much superior force . . ." There can be no doubt that the successful defense of Fort Ridgely and New Ulm saved towns farther down river from attack, and may have settled the outcome of the Sioux Uprising, though it was by no means over.

NEW ULM CITIZENS, *led by Flandrau, evacuated the town on August 25, 1862. About two thousand refugees walked or rode from New Ulm to Mankato.* SCENE FROM GÁG-HELLER-SCHWENDINGER PANORAMA.

9.

ENCOUNTER AT BIRCH COULEE

THE BIRCH COULEE BATTLEFIELD *is a rolling prairie that still looks much as it did in 1862. This view, looking toward the ravine, shows the author standing about where the troops camped when they were attacked.* PHOTO BY LUCILE CARLEY.

AFTER the successful defense of Fort Ridgely and New Ulm, a second phase of the Indian war began—an organized military effort to defeat and punish the Sioux and secure the release of their many captives. To do this, Sibley eventually would be reinforced by other units, but when he arrived at Ridgely his "army" consisted principally of some 940 fresh recruits in the ten companies of the untried Sixth Minnesota Regiment (commanded by Colonel William Crooks of St. Paul) and about four hundred volunteer cavalrymen under Colonel McPhail. The latter included two hundred members of the Cullen Frontier Guards raised by Major William J. Cullen, former northern superintendent of Indian affairs.

This was the only time during the Sioux Uprising that Sibley had under his command any appreciable number of mounted men. Since they were volunteers who had not formally enlisted for any set period of time, many of them soon decided to take their horses and return home to harvest the year's crops. Their departure left Sibley with the impossible task of locating the mounted Sioux with an unwieldy army of infantry.

Moreover, the quality of Sibley's foot soldiers was doubtful. The commander himself was forced to check nightly to see that his pickets remained awake. His officers held daily drills to strengthen the green infantry forces and to familiarize the men with the miscellaneous collection of small arms provided them. At the time of the uprising, Adjutant General Oscar Malmros reported that most of the state's good firearms had gone with earlier regiments to the Civil War and that he had on hand about four thousand old small arms. Many of these were of foreign manufacture, and the adjutant general found that the ammunition he was able to procure frequently did not fit them. At one point, Malmros became so desperate that he converted water pipe into needed bullets. Sibley himself sent repeated pleas to the state's officials for Springfield rifles and mounted troops.

While Sibley attempted to equip and train his soldiers, relatives and friends of settlers killed by the Indians reminded the colonel that the bodies still lay unburied where they had fallen. Thus on August 31, after scouts assured him that no large band of Sioux stalked nearby, Sibley sent out a burial party from Fort Ridgely. It was composed of Company A of the Sixth Minnesota under Captain Hiram P. Grant, some fifty mounted men of the Cullen Guards under Captain Joseph Anderson, seventeen teamsters and wagons, and a fatigue detail of other soldiers and settlers—a total of about 170 men. Included were Agent Galbraith, a few citizens who wanted to look for the bodies of relatives, and Dr. Jared W. Daniels, former Upper Agency physician who was now assistant surgeon of the Sixth Minnesota.

The entire party was commanded by Brown, the former Indian agent, who had become a major in the volunteer army. (In later years a controversy developed over whether Brown or Grant was in command. In spite of the fact that the inscription on the Birch Coulee State Monument near Morton names Grant as the commander, the evidence—notably Sibley's own statements—buttresses Brown's claim to this dubious distinction.) In addition to burying bodies, Brown was instructed to find out, if he could, where the Indians had gone and what they were up to. He had a personal interest in obtaining this information, since his wife and family were captives of the Sioux. Although Brown knew the country well and was a master of Indian signs, Sibley explicitly cautioned him not to camp near a mound or ravine where the Sioux could surprise him.

The major left the fort about 10:00 A.M. on August 31, moving slowly over the road to Redwood Ferry and stopping from time to

CAPTAIN JOSEPH ANDERSON (*far left*), *a veteran of the Mexican War and a resident of Minnesota since 1855, led the cavalry company that fought at Birch Coulee. Like his friend Major Brown, Anderson objected to the vulnerable location of the camp site.* PHOTO BY OLIVER, OKLAHOMA CITY, OKLAHOMA, 1863.

MAJOR JOSEPH R. BROWN *commanded the burial party that was almost wiped out at Birch Coulee. Although he did not approve of the camp site Grant selected, Brown did not insist that the troops move because he believed there were no Sioux in the area.* FROM A DAGUERREOTYPE TAKEN IN THE 1850s.

41

time to bury at least sixteen settlers. Although some accounts contain grim descriptions of the mutilation of bodies among these early victims, Dr. Daniels stated unequivocally: "I saw every one that was buried and not one was scalped or mutilated." It seems probable that the condition of the bodies, which had lain in the hot sun for nearly two weeks, gave rise to some false charges of mutilation. Brown's men bivouacked the first night on the Minnesota bottoms near the mouth of Birch Coulee Creek.

Early the next morning the forces divided. Brown crossed the Minnesota with Captain Anderson and his cavalry, while Grant and his infantry stayed on the north side. At the Lower Agency, Brown and his men found several corpses and buried them. Nathan Myrick located the body of his brother Andrew. Then Myrick and some other civilians returned to Fort Ridgely.

Brown's detachment scouted on up the south side of the river to Little Crow's abandoned village. A careful examination of the place convinced the major, Galbraith, Jack Frazer, veteran trader Alexander Faribault, and others in the party familiar with Sioux ways, that no Indians had been about for at least four days. Brown decided the Sioux must have gone to the Upper Agency or beyond and thus did not constitute a threat to his command.

Meanwhile Grant's infantry on the north side of the river found and buried the remains of Peter Quinn and some twenty of Marsh's soldiers who had been ambushed at Redwood Ferry. Grant's force then moved up the valley as far as Beaver Creek in Renville County, burying a number of bodies along the way. Near the stream the men came upon Mrs. Krieger, who had been wounded and left for dead when the Indians ambushed the Kitzman party on August 19. Mrs. Krieger had wandered about the area for thirteen days. Dr. Daniels treated her wounds and fixed up a bed for her in one of the wagons.

At Beaver Creek, Grant and his party, including Mrs. Krieger, turned back, cutting across the prairie eastward to a camp site he selected near Birch Coulee. Here he was joined near sunset by Brown's forces, returning from their expedition on the opposite side of the river. Together the two detachments had buried fifty-four up-

THE PAINTING *below shows the soldiers at Birch Coulee firing a volley at Indians emerging from the ravine in the background.* SCENE FROM GÁG-HELLER-SCHWENDINGER PANORAMA.

rising victims during the day. Neither group had seen any Indians.

The Sioux, however, were not as remote as Brown supposed. He was right in thinking that they had retreated beyond the Yellow Medicine River after their repulse at New Ulm. But this move had been deliberate. Its purpose was to put the warriors' families in a safer area and to woo the support of the Upper Sioux tribes. On September 1, the very day that Brown sought to locate them, the Indians were launching two ambitious forays. Little Crow led a raiding force of about 110 braves northeastward toward settlements on the edge of the Big Woods, while about 350 Indians under Gray Bird, his chief warrior, headed down the south side of the Minnesota River. Little Crow's forces intended to do some plundering and, if possible, threaten the rear of Sibley's army at Fort Ridgely and perhaps capture its provisions as they came in. Eventually, if all went as planned, Gray Bird's warriors were to cross the river and join Little Crow for further moves against the settlements farther down the valley.

THE RAVINE *from which Mankato's forces attacked the soldiers' camp is today a pleasant picnic area in Birch Coulee State Historic Site.* PHOTO BY BECKER.

Somehow Gray Bird's party and Brown's reconnoitering force missed actually encountering each other during the day. An advance group of Indians, however, reached Little Crow's village in time to see Anderson's cavalry moving off eastward across the prairie. The Indian scouts followed and learned that the soldiers were camping for the night near Birch Coulee. Unaware of the presence of Grant's infantry, the Sioux thought the cavalry was alone, that it could be easily surrounded at night and destroyed in the morning.

The camp site selected by Grant and accepted by Brown in what is now Birch Coulee State Historic Site was near wood and water but had little else to recommend it. The Indians could approach within gunshot from all sides and still be under cover. The camp itself, said Brown in his official report, "was made in the usual way." It was located some two hundred yards from the timber along the coulee, "with the wagons parked around the camp, and the team horses fastened to the wagons." The soldiers had what amounted to a corral less than a hundred yards in diameter with the tents inside the circle. Although Brown's party did not expect trouble, ten pickets were stationed around the camp. Located only about thirty yards out, however, they were too close to be effective.

While the soldiers slept, some two hundred warriors led by Gray Bird, Red Legs, Big Eagle, and Mankato crossed the river and encircled the camp under cover of darkness. Red Legs's men occupied steep-sided Birch Coulee to the east, while Big Eagle's band gathered behind a knoll on the prairie to the west. On the north, Gray Bird's braves approached through the grass. Mankato's warriors were divided between the coulee and a swale to the south.

Just before dawn on September 2, Anderson's cook noticed that the horses seemed restless. He awakened Anderson, and the two men were talking about the matter when Private William L. Hart, a sentinel facing the coulee, made out Indians moving in the grass and raised the alarm by firing at them. Hart then ran to safety in the corral, but his fellow lookout, Private Richard Gibbons, fell mortally wounded.

The Indians immediately poured a deadly fire into the partially awakened camp, wounding at least thirty men or so in the first few minutes. Anderson ordered his soldiers to take cover behind the

43

THE BIRCH COULEE MONUMENT (*foreground*), *erected by the state in 1894, rests not on the battlefield, but on a bluff overlooking Morton. Not only is it incorrectly located, but its legend names Grant rather than Brown as the leader of the troops. The monument in the background honors six Sioux who saved the lives of whites during the uprising.* PHOTO BY BECKER.

wagons, but Grant at first tried to form his men for a volley. Before long, however, the whites found positions from which they could keep the Indians at bay. Since most of the horses were killed early in the action, the men used the carcasses as effective barricades.

The heaviest fighting lasted about an hour, and Brown's party suffered most of its casualties during that time. The major, Anderson, and Galbraith were wounded, so Grant directed the strengthening of the camp's defenses when the Indian fire slackened. With only four shovels and their bayonets, knives, and tin plates, the men dug shallow rifle pits. As the day wore on, the attack lost much of its momentum, but the Indians continued their siege.

Meanwhile, sounds of the battle carried down the valley to Fort Ridgely, sixteen miles away. Hearing them, Sibley promptly sent out a relief party of 240 men under the leadership of Colonel McPhail. It was composed of Companies B, D, and E of the Sixth Minnesota, fifty mounted rangers, and a section of artillery. During the afternoon, the besieged soldiers at Birch Coulee were heartened by the sound of cannon fire as McPhail's forces approached. Near the main coulee, they encountered a detachment of Indians who made a lively demonstration. Thinking himself "almost completely surrounded," McPhail pulled back, set up a corral, and sent Lieutenant Sheehan back to Fort Ridgely for reinforcements.

As soon as Sheehan delivered McPhail's message, Sibley quickly left the fort with his entire remaining force of six companies of the Sixth regiment and two newly arrived companies of the Seventh. He reached McPhail's bivouac shortly after midnight, rested until daybreak, and then moved toward the beleaguered camp, shelling the area as he went. The artillery fire dispersed the outnumbered Sioux, and Colonel Sibley rode into Brown's camp about 11:00 A.M. on September 3.

There he found a "sickening sight." Thirteen men and no less than ninety horses lay dead, forty-seven men were severely wounded, and many more were less seriously hurt. Four of them later died of their wounds. The stench of decaying bodies was overwhelming. The survivors were weak and exhausted, having withstood a thirty-one hour siege largely without water and food. Tents were riddled with bullets, and debris littered the camp. Throughout the battle, Mrs. Krieger had kept to her wagon, the only one left upright. It was a tempting target, and there were two hundred bullet holes in the blankets and robes wrapped around her. Nevertheless, she escaped serious injury. Sibley's men gave the dead temporary burial at Birch Coulee. Then they placed the wounded in wagons and started for Fort Ridgely, reaching the post about midnight.

In the battle of Birch Coulee, the troops suffered the heaviest military casualties of the war. Big Eagle later reported that he had seen only two dead Indians. Some historians have surmised that the action at Birch Coulee may have diverted the Sioux from the down-river settlements toward which they were headed. On the other hand, events there taught the whites the folly of moving in hostile Indian territory without a large, well-trained army.

THE FOREST CITY STOCKADE, *where some 240 people took refuge, was built in twenty-four hours. It was one of a series of forts erected by Minnesota settlers for protection against Indian attacks.* DRAWING BY JOHN BODIN, IN *Condensed History of Meeker County* (LITCHFIELD, 1939).

WHILE Gray Bird's war party moved down the Minnesota Valley toward Birch Coulee on September 1, Little Crow and his braves made their way toward Forest City and Hutchinson. On the second day out, some seventy-five warriors openly disagreed with Little Crow's plan of action and went their own way. Eager to plunder towns as far eastward as possible, they were led by Walker Among Sacred Stones, the old head warrior of the Kaposia band. That night the mutinous faction encamped two miles northeast of the Robinson Jones place, where the Sioux Uprising had started three weeks earlier. Little Crow and his remaining thirty-five warriors camped two miles southeast of the Jones homestead.

Unaware of the presence of the Dakota nearby, Captain Richard Strout of Minneapolis with about fifty-five newly recruited men of Company B of the Tenth Minnesota (later the Ninth) and some twenty citizens camped that night right in the Jones yard. The soldiers, who had been sent to protect the Meeker County settlers, were en route to Forest City from Glencoe.

At Forest City, Captain George C. Whitcomb commanded a volunteer company that had skirmished with Indians north of Acton the previous day. When he learned of Strout's position, Whitcomb sent three mounted men to warn him of his peril. The riders, led by Jesse V. Branham, reached the camp at 3:00 A.M., found it completely unguarded, and spread the alarm. The soldiers spent the rest of the night hammering and cutting down Minié balls into bullets for their Belgian muskets.

Strout broke camp at daylight on September 3. After marching about two miles to the west shore of Hope Lake, the company came upon Little Crow's party (which the chief's half brother, White Spider, is said to have been leading at the time), and a running battle ensued. The other Indian faction under Walker Among Sacred Stones came up and helped surround Strout. The captain elected to fight his way out. With fixed bayonets the main body of the soldiers, led by Lieutenant William A. Clark, charged through Little Crow's lines and beat a hasty retreat to Hutchinson. Six soldiers were killed and at least fifteen (and perhaps as many as twenty-three) were wounded in this affair, which has been called the battle of Acton.

Early on the morning of September 4, Little Crow's reunited band, increased in strength by the arrival of twenty Upper Sioux the night

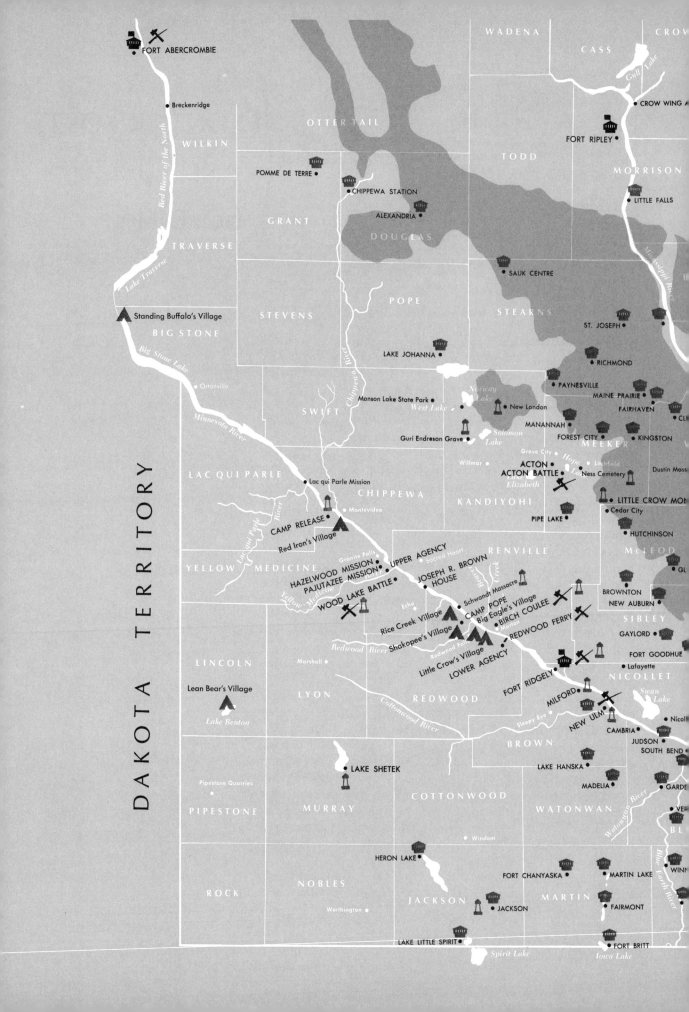

WADENA
CASS
CROW

FORT ABERCROMBIE

• Breckenridge

OTTER TAIL

TODD

FORT RIPLEY

• CROW WING

MORRISON

WILKIN

POMME DE TERRE

• LITTLE FALLS

CHIPPEWA STATION

TRAVERSE

GRANT

ALEXANDRIA

DOUGLAS

• SAUK CENTRE

STEARNS

St. JOSEPH

STEVENS

POPE

Standing Buffalo's Village

BIG STONE

• Ortonville

LAKE JOHANNA

• RICHMOND

MEEKER

• PAYNESVILLE

MAINE PRAIRIE

FAIRHAVEN

CL

Monson Lake State Park •

Norway Lake

• New London

MANANNAH

FOREST CITY

KINGSTON

Minnesota River

SWIFT

West Lake

Guri Endreson Grave •

Solomon Lake

Willmar •

Grove City

Hope

Litchfield

Dustin Mass

LAC QUI PARLE

Lac qui Parle Mission •

CHIPPEWA

ACTON

ACTON BATTLE

Ness Cemetery

LITTLE CROW MON

• Montevideo

KANDIYOHI

Lake Elizabeth

• Cedar City

CAMP RELEASE

Red Iron's Village

PIPE LAKE

HUTCHINSON

McLEOD

YELLOW MEDICINE

Granite Falls

Sacred Heart

RENVILLE

GL

HAZELWOOD MISSION

UPPER AGENCY

JOSEPH R. BROWN HOUSE

PAJUTAZEE MISSION

WOOD LAKE BATTLE

Schwandt Massacre

BROWNTON

NEW AUBURN

Echo

CAMP POPE

Big Eagle's Village

SIBLEY

Rice Creek Village

BIRCH COULEE

GAYLORD

Shakopee's Village

REDWOOD FERRY

FORT GOODHUE

Redwood River

Little Crow's Village

LOWER AGENCY

• Lafayette

LINCOLN

• Marshall

NICOLLET

Lean Bear's Village

LYON

REDWOOD

FORT RIDGELY

MILFORD

Swan Lake

• Nicol

Lake Benton

Cottonwood River

BROWN

Sleepy Eye •

NEW ULM

CAMBRIA

JUDSON

Pipestone Quarries

LAKE SHETEK

LAKE HANSKA

SOUTH BEND

MADELIA

GARDE

PIPESTONE

MURRAY

COTTONWOOD

WATONWAN

VER

BL

Windom •

HERON LAKE

FORT CHANYASKA

MARTIN LAKE

WINN

ROCK

NOBLES

JACKSON

MARTIN

Worthington •

• JACKSON

FAIRMONT

LAKE LITTLE SPIRIT

Spirit Lake

FORT BRITT

Iowa Lake

DAKOTA TERRITORY

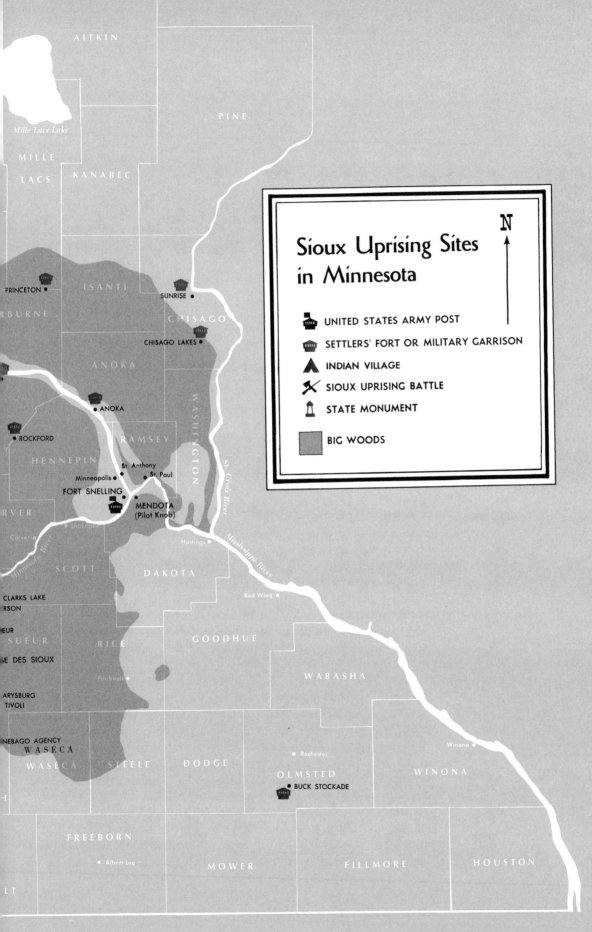

AITKIN

PINE

Mille Lacs Lake

MILLE LACS

KANABEC

ISANTI

SUNRISE ●

PRINCETON ●

CHISAGO

CHISAGO LAKES ●

BURNE

ANOKA

WASHINGTON

ANOKA ●

ROCKFORD ●

RAMSEY

St. Croix River

HENNEPIN

St. Anthony

Minneapolis ●   ● St. Paul

FORT SNELLING

MENDOTA
(Pilot Knob)

RVER

Shakopee

Carver ●

Minnesota River

Mississippi River

SCOTT

DAKOTA

Hastings ●

CLARKS LAKE

RSON

Red Wing ●

EUR

SUEUR

RICE

GOODHUE

GE DES SIOUX

Faribault ●

ARYSBURG
TIVOLI

WABASHA

NEBAGO AGENCY
WASECA

Rochester ●

Winona ●

WASECA

STEELE

DODGE

OLMSTED

WINONA

● BUCK STOCKADE

FREEBORN

Albert Lea ●

MOWER

FILLMORE

HOUSTON

LT

IOWA

Legend

Sioux Uprising Sites
in Minnesota

N ↑

UNITED STATES ARMY POST

SETTLERS' FORT OR MILITARY GARRISON

INDIAN VILLAGE

SIOUX UPRISING BATTLE

STATE MONUMENT

BIG WOODS

CAPTAIN RICHARD STROUT'S *inexperienced volunteers fought in hand-to-hand combat with Little Crow's warriors in the battle of Acton.* SCENE FROM GÁG-HELLER-SCHWENDINGER PANORAMA.

before, again divided into two parties for attacks on Forest City and Hutchinson. At both places the Indians were foiled by settlers securely positioned within stockades. The warriors had to content themselves with plundering and burning houses and killing a few people who had not sought shelter in the fortifications. By late afternoon the Indians abandoned their efforts, and on September 5 the two groups departed for Yellow Medicine.

The settlers had contrasting reactions to Little Crow's raid into the Big Woods. For many it sparked a hurried exodus from the area; for others it only confirmed their resolution to defend their homes at any cost. Typical of the latter were the citizens of Forest City, who, learning that the Sioux were in the vicinity, built a stockade in twenty-four hours — finishing it just in time to repel the attack mentioned above. Fortifications were also built in other settlements north of the Minnesota River. (See map on pages 46–47.) These shelters usually were simple stockades ten or twelve feet high and about a hundred feet square, with loopholes to shoot through.

There were, however, some interesting variations in the chain of settlers' forts that soon stretched from Little Falls to Glencoe. At Maine Prairie, for example, an isolated band of farmers built a sturdy two-story fort with a double row of timbers. Defenders of St. Joseph erected three pentagonal blockhouses of green timber a foot thick. At nearby St. Cloud was "Fort Holes," one of three fortifications in the town and among the strongest on the frontier. It was circular, forty-five feet in diameter, and sported a bulletproof tower with holes for sharpshooters. No attack ever tested the fort, which was intended as a stronghold for inhabitants of St. Cloud's lower town near the Mississippi River. Hutchinson's post, completed on August 27, had a timber stockade eight feet high and sheltered over four hundred people during the attack on

September 4. Settlers at Sauk Centre hastily erected a stockade of tamarack logs which was later converted by soldiers into a substantial fort. At Clearwater, on the Mississippi below St. Cloud, the inhabitants formed a home guard and built a substantial defensive fort. And at Little Falls the citizens fortified the Morrison County courthouse so that women and children could sleep there at night. The men camped and did guard duty outside the structure and farmed the fields in detachments during the daytime.

The citizen-soldiers who held forth at these various improvised forts around the state usually took such names as "guards," "rifles," and "rangers." But others like the St. Peter Frontier Avengers and the Le Sueur Tigers, both of whom took part in the second battle at New Ulm, adopted more aggressive sobriquets. One group had an ethnic connection — the Scandinavian Guards of Nicollet County whom Sibley left to garrison St. Peter after he departed to raise the siege of Fort Ridgely.

South of the Minnesota River, too, defense measures were begun which led to the formation of a state militia. On August 28, Governor Ramsey authorized Flandrau to take command of troops along the state's southern and southwestern frontiers. Commissioned a colonel in Minnesota's volunteer militia on September 3, Flandrau set up headquarters at South Bend, four miles southwest of Mankato. He immediately established planned defense lines with forts at close intervals from New Ulm to the Iowa border. The principal works, all of which were garrisoned by soldiers under his command, were at New Ulm, Garden City, Winnebago, Blue Earth, Martin Lake, Madelia, and Marysburg. At villages where women and children still remained, these fortifications were generally constructed of earth or logs, with houses inside to shelter the noncombatants in case of attack. The structures were usually square with bastions at the corners. The rude posts communicated not only with each other but with a fort at Iowa Lake on the border. The latter was manned by the Iowa Northern Border Brigade, which also garrisoned additional Iowa forts to the west and south.

At Madelia the men commanded by E. St. Julien Cox, who earlier had led a force to New Ulm, built an "artistic fortification" on a commanding site. Named Fort Cox after the captain, it was an octagonal,

SAUK CENTRE'S STURDY STOCKADE *of tamarack logs was in 1863 a stout fortification enclosing three acres and armed with howitzers. Troops were stationed until 1865 at this major post on the important supply line from St. Cloud to Fort Abercrombie.* OIL PAINTED IN 1864. SAUK CENTRE PUBLIC LIBRARY.

49

two-story structure surrounded by a breastwork and a moat six feet deep and four feet wide at the bottom. At other points rifle pits were dug and temporary earthworks thrown up. Rude though they were, the defenses effectively deterred the Dakota, although roving bands still occasionally attacked isolated settlers. On September 10, for example, a party of perhaps twenty Indians terrorized settlers in the valley of Butternut Creek in northwestern Blue Earth County. The Dakota killed one man and wounded another at a house where twenty-two members of a Welsh colony had congregated and then went on to murder three more farmers and wound others at various spots in the general area. Word of these encounters reached nearby forts, but the Indians escaped the ineffectual pursuit.

Another area where fear of Indian raids was translated into action was the St. Croix Valley. Citizens there were alarmed both by news of the widespread Sioux raids and by rumors that the Chippewa of the Mississippi under Chief Hole-in-the-Day might join their traditional enemies to swoop down on the St. Croix settlements. Volunteer units were raised for defense at Stillwater (Frontier Guards, Captain D. Bronson, Jr.), Sunrise (Chisago County Rangers, Captain James Starkey), Marine (Marine Guards, Captain Robert Rich), Taylors Falls, and others places. The Ramsey Picket Guards, a group of mounted men captained by George W. Few of Little Canada, rode northward in September. Named commander of all the St. Croix Valley volunteer militia was Colonel Francis R. Delano, former warden of the territorial prison. In the Chisago Lakes area, citizens built earthen breastworks and moved in a cannon from St. Paul to defend Center City, while volunteer soldiers at Sunrise built temporary quarters of logs.

Although some St. Croix citizens thought they saw Indians and panic briefly spread through Stillwater, no raids occurred. The Sioux were far to the south and west, but for a time the Chippewa did pose a distinct threat. On August 18, 1862, the very day the Sioux Uprising began at the Lower Agency, Chippewa Agent Lucius C. Walker heard disturbing news at agency headquarters on the north bank of the Crow Wing River three miles from its junction with the Mississippi. He was told that Chippewa warriors were gathering at Gull Lake to the north. Fearing an attack on the agency, Walker sent for military help from Fort Ripley, the regular army post located on the west bank of the Mississippi about seven miles downstream from the mouth of the Crow Wing. First constructed in 1848, the fort consisted of small one-story buildings arranged on three sides of a square; the fourth side was open to the Mississippi River. At the time it was garrisoned by only thirty Fifth Minnesota soldiers under Lieutenant Frank B. Fobes. (Captain Francis Hall was absent on leave, and it will be remembered that Lieutenant Timothy J. Sheehan and fifty men had been sent to Fort Ridgely.)

Fobes left a handful of men at the fort and with twenty others headed for Crow Wing village. At this settlement on the east bank of the Mississippi near its junction with the Crow Wing, the troops met Walker, who had abandoned the agency and was fleeing in nervous haste toward Ripley. Convinced that Hole-in-the-Day was the main troublemaker, Walker ordered Fobes to arrest the wily, defiant chief,

LUCIUS C. WALKER *was agent for the Chippewa of the Mississippi from May, 1861, until August 22, 1862, when he killed himself while fleeing from the unruly Chief Hole-in-the-Day and his followers. The Vermont-born Walker had earlier served as a Republican representative in Minnesota's first state legislature and as a dealer in real estate.* FROM AMBROTYPE OF FIRST LEGISLATURE, 1858.

whose government-built house stood nearby. Hole-in-the-Day escaped across the river with his three wives in the face of shots from soldiers' guns and joined the Chippewa assembled at Gull Lake.

Meanwhile, Big Boy, a leader of the Pillager band of Chippewa at Leech Lake and a friend of the whites, arrived at Fort Ripley with a warning of a possible attack on both the agency and the fort. His people, he said, held seven whites in captivity. They had looted private and government buildings at Leech Lake, stolen horses, and killed some cattle and were set to join Hole-in-the-Day, whom Big Boy disliked, at Gull Lake.

The post commander, Captain Hall, hurried back from his leave, declared martial law over the surrounding territory, and warned the settlers to flee to Fort Ripley for protection. More than 150, mostly women and children, responded, but they were not greatly comforted by the post's weak defenses, small garrison, and shortage of ammunition. Fortunately, no attack came. In a few days a company of the Sixth Minnesota Regiment and two companies of the Seventh arrived to bolster the fort's man power.

After leaving Crow Wing, Agent Walker became increasingly distraught over what he thought was a general Chippewa outbreak. As a

result, he determined to take his family to St. Paul. When he reached St. Cloud, he met William P. Dole, United States commissioner of Indian affairs, and his party who had been sent to negotiate a treaty with the Red Lake and Pembina Chippewa. Undeterred, Walker continued his journey. By the time he reached the vicinity of Monticello on August 22, he was so deranged that he shot and killed himself.

Dole returned to St. Paul to confer with Governor Ramsey and then decided to try to lessen the danger of warfare by holding a council with Hole-in-the-Day. Arriving at Fort Ripley on August 29 with a military escort of two of the companies sent to reinforce the post, Dole tried to arrange a meeting with the elusive chief. When the council finally took place, it was held at Crow Wing in the presence of "some two hundred" of Hole-in-the-Day's followers in war attire. Dole soon lost patience with the truculent chief and decided to return to St. Paul. First, however, he instructed special agent Ashley C. Morrill to try to bring matters to a head by discontinuing provisions for the Indians.

Left without supplies, Hole-in-the-Day formulated a plan to attack the agency to secure the provisions there. In a stormy meeting of the Chippewa, Hole-in-the-Day's fellow chiefs rejected his plan. They did not wish to face the three companies of infantry by then on the scene. The Chippewa therefore returned some stolen property, and 364 Pillagers departed for their homes at Leech Lake. But Hole-in-the-Day, undiscouraged by the departure of his colleagues, refused to relinquish his warlike plans unless the whites provided $10,000 worth of goods. He was refused, and the disturbance quieted down.

Only two of the eight Chippewa bands had taken any part in the episode, and Hole-in-the-Day may have been bluffing, at least in part, in an unsuccessful effort to extort a new and more liberal treaty as well as payment of long-standing claims. There is some evidence that the Chippewa chief and Little Crow may have had a personal understanding to attack the whites simultaneously, but it is doubtful that their followers, who had so long been enemies, would have tolerated an effective alliance. Had such an agreement been implemented, however, the dimensions of the war would have been greatly extended, and the hastily recruited militia forces in their log forts would have faced a far graver problem.

The men in the various state militia units served only a few days in some cases and as long as two and a half months in others. Some of the citizen-soldier groups were relieved in mid-September by regular United States army troops of the Twenty-fifth Wisconsin Regiment, commanded by Colonel Milton Montgomery, and others in mid-October by the Twenty-seventh Iowa Infantry. Montgomery was ordered to supplant Flandrau as commander of the southwestern sector. The stay of these "outsiders" was brief, however, for early in the winter they were sent south to fight in the Civil War along with the Third Minnesota. Then the job of defending the frontier fell to the Sixth, Seventh, Eighth, Ninth, and Tenth Minnesota Volunteers and the First Regiment of Minnesota Mounted Rangers, but this is getting ahead of the story. Some of these units took part in yet another episode that remains to be told — the Indians' lengthy harassment of a fort far to the west.

IN EARLY SEPTEMBER still another regular United States army post farther west on the edge of the Minnesota frontier was besieged by the Dakota for six weeks or so. It was Fort Abercrombie, located on the perimeter of the area's military defense line on the west bank of the Red River in Dakota Territory. Lieutenant Colonel John J. Abercrombie of the United States army had established the fort in 1858 at the approximate head of navigation on the Red River near present-day McCauleyville. The first site was subject to floods, so the fort was moved a short distance to drier ground and occupied by regular troops starting in 1860. After the Civil War began, Minnesota volunteers replaced the regulars manning the fort, which was intended to serve as a check on the Yankton Sioux and to spur white settlement in the Red River Valley. It also helped guard the burgeoning steamboat traffic on the Red River as well as wagon trains traveling overland from Minnesota to the gold fields of Montana.

The three regular army posts in the region — Forts Abercrombie, Ripley, and Ridgely — had many similarities. All three were forts in name only and ill-suited for defense. Lacking a stockade or blockhouses, Abercrombie consisted of three scattered buildings — a wooden barracks for enlisted men, wooden quarters for officers, and a small brick commissary — plus a small guardhouse, sutler's store, and stables. Like the nearby ravines at Fort Ridgely, bushes and other vegetation on both sides of the Red River gave the Indians good cover from which to fire on Fort Abercrombie. In another parallel with Ridgely, Abercrombie's shortcomings were also overcome in large measure by the presence of cannon and able artillerists, some of whom had been trained in Germany. Three twelve-pound mountain howitzers were to prove important in beating back Dakota attacks.

When the Sioux War broke out, Fort Abercrombie was garrisoned by Company D of the Fifth Minnesota Regiment (Ridgely was manned by the same outfit's Company B and Fort Ripley by Company C). Commanding Company D was German-born, aristocratic-looking Captain John Vander Horck, a thirty-one-year-old grocer and the village treasurer of West St. Paul. He had arrived at Abercrombie from Fort Snelling, some 225 miles away, on March 29, 1862, at the head of a company of at least seventy-eight men. In keeping with his orders, Vander Horck sent a detachment of thirty men, led by Lieutenant Francis A. Cariveau, to Fort Sanborn, a primitive post located about fifty miles to the north down the Red River near present-day Georgetown, where the troops were to guard installations of the Hudson's Bay Company and Burbank & Company.

Vander Horck and his men endured several months of typically dull outpost duty in a sparsely settled area. All that relieved the monotony were occasional visitors and the twice-a-week Burbank & Company stagecoach running between Georgetown and St. Cloud, the nearest community of any size some 150 miles to the southeast. There were few if any signs of Indian trouble; relations with both the Dakota and the Chippewa were amicable.

In July, 1862, however, Congress had set in motion plans to negotiate a land-cession treaty with the Pembina and Red Lake Chippewa bands. The treaty site was to be a spot at the forks of the Red and Red Lake

II.
THE SIEGE OF FORT ABERCROMBIE

CAPTAIN JOHN VANDER HORCK, *shown many years after the Sioux Uprising, was the controversial commander of the garrison at Fort Abercrombie.*

FORT ABERCROMBIE *was built on the west bank of the Red River at the head of navigation. Like Forts Ridgely and Ripley, it was garrisoned in 1862 by troops of the Fifth Minnesota Regiment and was ill-suited for defense. In this 1862 view from the north, the fort is shown to have grown into a collection of numerous small wooden buildings.* DRAWING BY SWEENY, 1862.

rivers near what is now Grand Forks, North Dakota. To treat with the Chippewa, Indian Commissioner William P. Dole and John G. Nicolay, Lincoln's private secretary whom the president sent to Minnesota to observe the negotiations, met in St. Cloud on the eve of the Sioux War. Soon after they headed off across the prairie toward the treaty site, they learned of the Dakota Uprising and the Chippewa disturbance and returned to St. Paul. The Chippewa treaty Dole and Nicolay intended to negotiate had to wait until 1863, but later in 1862, as has been seen, the two men and others did deal successfully with the disgruntled Chippewa Chief Hole-in-the-Day to restore calm in the Fort Ripley-Crow Wing area.

Meanwhile, in mid-August a treaty train of thirty wagons loaded with Indian goods and some two hundred cattle reached the vicinity of Fort Abercrombie on its way from St. Cloud to the proposed treaty site. The train was traveling ahead of Dole and Nicolay, and Vander Horck had orders to provide an escort for it. By August 23, when Vander Horck received new orders to detain the goods and cattle at Abercrombie, the train had already passed beyond the fort. With these orders came a clipping or proof sheet from a St. Cloud newspaper that gave the Abercrombie commander his first news of the Indian warfare. The wagons and herd were quickly returned to a corral near the fort, and Vander Horck also recalled the detachment he had sent to Georgetown. At least eighty citizens of the area, alerted by runners from the fort, came in for protection, some bringing their families. They were housed in the enlisted men's barracks and put to work, along with the soldiers, piling up cordwood and timber around the buildings and constructing emplacements for the howitzers.

Vander Horck was a cautious commander who wisely permitted very little roaming outside the fort to save cattle or for other purposes. (Jane Grey Swisshelm of the *St. Cloud Democrat* and others later criti-

cized him for being timid.) He did, however, send Lieutenant **John Groetch** with about a dozen men to reconnoiter as far as Breckenridge, fifteen miles to the south. They saw no Indians but found the mutilated bodies of three men, a woman, and a child in a Breckenridge hotel. The four-story structure was burned by Indians later the same evening. The scouting party also came upon a wounded, elderly woman, identified in some accounts as a Mrs. Scott and in others as a Mrs. Ryan, crawling near the riverbank. She said Indians had shot her, killed her son, and kidnaped her grandson from her home some fifteen miles east of Breckenridge. The troops took her back to Fort Abercrombie, where she eventually recovered from her wounds.

LINCOLN'S SECRETARY, *John G. Nicolay (standing), played the role of a gun-toting frontiersman in camp at Big Lake, Sherburne County, on August 24, 1862. He and Indian Commissioner William P. Dole (seated) were in Minnesota to negotiate a treaty with the Pembina and Red Lake Chippewa, but the Dakota War forced them to give up their trip to the Red River Valley. They did, however, treat with Hole-in-the-Day.* PHOTO FROM THE LINCOLN NATIONAL LIFE FOUNDATION COLLECTION, FORT WAYNE, INDIANA.

On August 23 Vander Horck dispatched to St. Paul two volunteer couriers — Walter P. Hills (who subsequently made two more such rides) and Elisha L. Spencer — to inform authorities of the situation at Abercrombie and to request reinforcements and ammunition. The latter was no routine request. Ever since the previous April, when the men discovered that the fort stocked only the wrong size ammunition for its .69-caliber muskets, Vander Horck had been requesting 20,000 rounds of the proper cartridges. Although they were promised, none materialized by the time of the Indian attacks.

While the garrison grew increasingly weary from constant vigilance and sentry duty, all was reasonably quiet until August 30 when a small band of Dakota made a bold raid and successfully drove off most of the considerable stock grazing on the prairie as far as a mile from the fort. Vander Horck would permit no one to take off after the Indians, but the next day a scouting party recovered forty to fifty head of cattle.

In the early morning of September 3, Vander Horck was inspecting the outside picket line, probably to keep the sentries awake, when one of them mistook him for an Indian and shot him in the arm. While his wound was being dressed at daybreak, an Indian force of perhaps a hundred warriors, some of them mounted, attacked the fort. They concentrated on the south side, where stables outside the barricade presented an inviting target. In fact, it soon became clear that the attackers were mainly interested in securing horses that would help them maintain a siege. With Vander Horck wounded and Lieutenant Cariveau sick, Lieutenant Groetch took command. Burning haystacks shed a grotesque light over the whole scene as the garrison managed to repulse the Indians after two hours of fighting. Cannon fire helped, but so did the intense efforts of armed citizens, bent on saving their animals from capture. They were led by Captain T. D. Smith, the post quartermaster. He was given much of the credit for the defeat of the Indians, who kept up desultory firing for several hours from the dense cover along the river. Casualties were light. Two whites were wounded, one of whom died. Two Indians were found dead after the fight, but perhaps four more were thought to have been killed and as many as fifteen wounded.

After the battle, the garrison learned to its dismay that only 350 rounds of .69-caliber bullets were left. Women joined in meeting the crisis by taking .69-caliber balls from cases of canister for the cannon in order to secure enough musket ammunition to withstand another attack. It was not long in coming.

About daybreak on September 6 the Indians launched their heaviest assault on the fort. Although Vander Horck and others estimated that the Indian force contained several hundred, it probably did not number more than 125 to 150 warriors, perhaps drawn from the Upper Sioux Sisseton band, plus some Wahpeton. During Sisseton and Wahpeton claims trials that dragged on in later years, these bands denied taking part in the war. Members of the garrison, however, said they recognized the well-known Sisseton leader, Sweet Corn, among the attackers.

At any rate, on September 6 the Indians at first concentrated again on the stables and managed to enter them, only to be dislodged after ten minutes of heavy fighting. They then came at the fort from all sides, with the hottest contest being near the commissary building. Well-directed cannon fire broke up any concentrations the Indians attempted, however, and after several hours of futile fighting the attackers retired to the cover along the riverbank. Garrison casualties totaled two men killed and one wounded. Indian casualties, as usual, were said to be much higher, maybe twenty killed. Joseph Demarais, the post's mixed-blood interpreter, later learned that Indian losses were so heavy that they gave up attempts to take the fort by assault and settled for continued harassment with sniping fire from a distance. Their targets included members of the garrison who went down to the river for water, since, like Ridgely, Abercrombie had no well.

Vander Horck repeatedly sent messengers to St. Paul asking for help. Although no word got back to him, assistance slowly took shape in the form of a relief force to lift the siege. On September 6 Governor Ramsey ordered the relief expedition to set out under the leadership of Captain Emil A. Buerger, a veteran of the Prussian army and a member of a Minnesota sharpshooter company, who had been wounded in the Civil War and returned to the state in a prisoner exchange. As it started from St. Paul en route to St. Cloud, Buerger's force consisted of about sixty men of the Third Minnesota under Sergeant Abraham F. Dearborn, Company D of the Seventh Minnesota under Captain Rolla Banks, and Company G of the Eighth Minnesota under Captain George Atkinson. A fieldpiece under Lieutenant R. J. McHenry caught up two days later.

Meanwhile, three other units had been on guard for some time in the St. Cloud–Sauk Centre area. They were Company H of the Eighth Minnesota under Captain George C. McCoy, Company G of the Ninth Minnesota under Captain Theodore H. Barrett, and a small company of mounted citizens (called the Northern Rangers) commanded by Captain Ambrose Freeman. McCoy was under orders to stay in the Sauk Centre region, but Barrett and Freeman on their own responsibility had started for Abercrombie with their men when they received orders from Buerger to wait for his expedition at Wyman's Station near Alexandria. When these groups were combined on September 19, they totaled about 450 men. They reached Abercrombie on the afternoon of September 23 to the joy of the harassed garrison and its besieged citizens.

But Vander Horck did not know the relief expedition was coming, and this caused one more unfortunate episode on the morning of September 23. Feeling increasingly desperate, the commander dispatched another messenger toward St. Paul, accompanied part of the way by an escort of twenty men. The escort was returning when Indians fired from ambush about a mile from the fort and killed two of the party. A detachment sent out the next day found the two bodies badly mutilated. Vander Horck was severely criticized by some of the garrison for this loss of life. In the long siege, however, total casualties at the fort amounted to only five dead and five wounded. Historian Folwell, for one, was disposed to give credit for the light casualties to Vander Horck's "husbandry of his command."

There was a skirmish with the Indians on September 26 and again on September 29, the date usually given for the real end of the siege. The next day the Third Minnesota detachment and Freeman's cavalry escorted some sixty men, women, and children on a wagon trip to St. Cloud. The settlers reached that city safely five days later. Company D of the Fifth Minnesota was soon sent to join other Minnesota units fighting in the Civil War. Vander Horck, however, remained at Fort Abercrombie to oversee its improvement. Soldiers cut down the brush and trees that had afforded the Indians convenient cover, and by February, 1863, they had erected three blockhouses as well as a stockade on all but the river side. Fort Abercrombie continued to guard the edge of the Minnesota frontier and to serve as a supply base for wagon train expeditions to the Montana gold fields throughout the 1860s. The post was finally abandoned in 1877 and fell into neglect. It was partially reconstructed in 1938 under the auspices of the Works Progress Administration and is now a North Dakota state historic site.

AFTER THE SIEGE, *Fort Abercrombie looked more like a fort with the addition of a stockade, blockhouses, and several buildings.* SKETCH BY GEORGE K. ELSBURY, SEVENTH MINNESOTA REGIMENT, MAY, 1863.

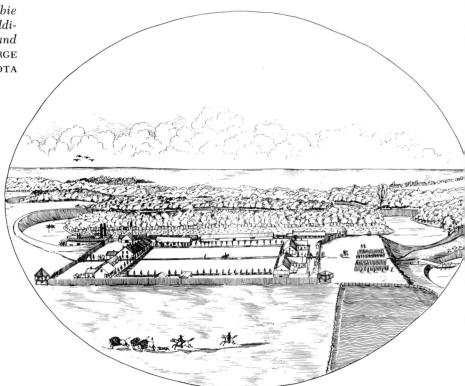

After the battles of Birch Coulee and Acton, the Big Woods raid, the various September attacks, and the protracted siege of Fort Abercrombie, the Sioux offensive ground to a halt. The initiative would now pass to the state's military forces as Sibley and Flandrau began to implement a plan formulated by Governor Ramsey. Flandrau and his successors were to hold the frontier with its chain of forts while Sibley moved against the Indians in the direction of Yellow Medicine. According to Ramsey, the over-all objectives of the plan were to free the settlers held captive by the Indians and to "exterminate" or drive the Dakota "forever beyond the borders of the state."

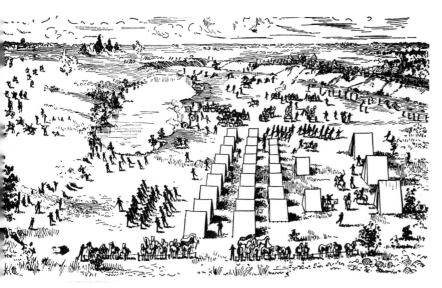

ARTIST'S CONCEPTION *of the battle of Wood Lake — the decisive encounter of the war.* FROM A. P. A. CONNOLLY, *Minnesota Massacre* (1896).

12.
DECISION AT WOOD LAKE

BEFORE the state's military forces could seize the initiative, it was necessary for Sibley to get his troops ready to move upriver from Fort Ridgely, where they had been headquartered since August 28. The colonel's preparations to march proceeded so deliberately that he was called a "snail," a coward, and the "State undertaker" or worse by newspaper editors and other citizens already irritated by his cautious march to the fort. Stung by the widespread criticism, Sibley on September 4 tried unsuccessfully to resign his commission. On the same day he wrote his wife about the complainers at home: "Well, let them come and fight these Indians themselves, and they will [have] something to do besides grumbling." Regardless of mounting pressure, he would not be stampeded into moving before he had the soldiers and supplies he felt essential to handle any Indian forces he might come up against.

The task of obtaining the men, arms, ammunition, and supplies required by Sibley fell largely to Adjutant General Malmros and Governor Ramsey, who bombarded the governors of other states, the war department in Washington, and President Lincoln with requests for help. At that time, however, the Civil War was going badly for the Union, and Lincoln appealed to the governors of the northern states for still more men. When Ramsey protested that Minnesota could not provide its quota of troops and needed an extension of the draft because of the uprising, Lincoln replied on August 27: "Attend to the Indians. If the draft cannot proceed of course it will not proceed. Necessity knows no law. The Government cannot extend the time."

By September 5 the Minnesota governor's pleas to Washington were still being more or less ignored. At five o'clock on the morning of September 6, Ramsey dispatched the following pointed telegram to the president: "Those Indian outrages continue. I asked Secretary [of War Edwin M.] Stanton to authorize the United States Quartermaster to purchase, say, 500 horses. He refuses. . . . This is not our

TO GOVERNOR ALEXANDER RAMSEY *fell the task of mobilizing Minnesota's resources to resist the onslaught of the Sioux. A blunt, energetic man, Ramsey went to Minnesota in 1849 as the first governor of the newly organized territory. Later he was to serve as United States senator and as secretary of war.* PHOTO TAKEN IN WASHINGTON, D.C., 1865.

war; it is a national war. . . . Answer me at once. More than 500 whites have been murdered by the Indians."

This time Ramsey got some action. Before the end of the day the war department named Major General John Pope commander of a newly created Military Department of the Northwest with headquarters at St. Paul. His appointment was looked upon by many as "banishment" for having lost the second battle of Bull Run, although earlier he had been a successful commander in the western theater of the Civil War. Pope's first letter of advice and instructions to Sibley, written from St. Paul on September 17, urged the colonel to push on and exterminate the Indians engaged in the outbreak.

Sibley had planned to march on September 2 but found his timetable upset again and again. The loss of over ninety horses at Birch Coulee was a serious setback, as was the departure for home of virtually all his remaining volunteer cavalry. By September 13 he had left only twenty-five mounted men. He was also bogged down by lack of experienced officers and disciplined soldiers.

The colonel was acutely aware that delay worked a hardship on the whites and mixed-bloods held prisoner by the Indians. He knew, too, that if he made a mistake in dealing with the Sioux, the captives would be killed. Thus the presence of so many of these helpless people in Indian camps in a way dictated his strategy.

Guessing that Little Crow might be growing tired of warring with the whites, Sibley decided to try to open negotiations. When he left the battlefield at Birch Coulee, he attached a message for the chief to an upright split stake. It read: "If Little Crow has any proposition to make to me, let him send a half-breed to me, and he shall be protected in and out of camp." Little Crow replied on September 7, explaining why the Indians began the war and seeming to hint that he would consider a proposition regarding the captives. To this Sibley made the brief answer: "You have murdered many of our people without sufficient cause. Return me the prisoners, under a flag of truce, and I will talk with you then like a man."

In subsequent communications Little Crow showed no inclination to give up the prisoners, while Sibley insisted on their return before he would entertain any proposals for peace. Without Little Crow's knowledge, the mixed-blood who delivered his last note to Sibley on September 12 also brought a letter from Chiefs Wabasha and Taopi in which they asked how they could arrange to be taken under Sibley's protection. The colonel replied that he would soon be on the march and that Indians who desired protection should gather with their captives on the prairie "in full sight of my troops" with a white flag "conspicuously displayed."

Sibley was heartened by this and other evidence he received of a division in the Indian ranks. He was assured, however, that Little Crow and his supporters still retained control over the main body of braves, who at that time were gathered at the mouth of the Chippewa River near present-day Montevideo awaiting the army's advance.

An eloquent rebuttal of the arguments of "friendlies" among the Dakota and for continuing the fighting apparently was delivered at an Indian council by Rdainyanka, Wabasha's son-in-law. Although some of the details of his speech are not substantiated elsewhere, it could well have turned the scales for continuing war, and it points up the precarious position of the captives. In his early book on the uprising, Isaac V. D. Heard recorded Rdainyanka's speech as follows:

"I am for continuing the war, and am opposed to the delivery of the prisoners. I have no confidence that the whites will stand by any agreement they make if we give them up. Ever since we treated with them their agents and traders have robbed and cheated us. Some of our people have been shot, some hung; others placed upon floating ice and drowned; and many have been starved in their prisons. It was not the intention of the [Dakota] nation to kill any of the whites until the four men returned from Acton and told what they had done. When they did this, all the young men became excited, and commenced the massacre. The older ones would have prevented it if they could, but since the treaties they have lost all their influence. We may regret what has happened, but the matter has gone too far to be remedied. We have got to die. Let us, then, kill as many of the whites as possible, and let the prisoners die with us."

Daily drills, particularly in skirmishing, whipped Sibley's green soldiers into a force he felt could be depended upon. An essential consignment of 50,000 cartridges arrived on September 11, and needed provisions and clothing came in on September 13 and 14. On the thirteenth, too, Sibley received his first experienced troops—270 infantrymen of the Third Minnesota Regiment who had seen action

GENERAL JOHN POPE *assumed command of the troops fighting the Sioux in September, 1862. A career army man, he fully understood the folly of chasing mounted Indians without cavalry.* FROM AN AMBROTYPE BY MATHEW BRADY TAKEN IN THE 1860s.

MANKATO (*Blue Earth*), *chief of a large band of Mdewakanton Sioux, was killed at Wood Lake on September 23, 1862, by a cannon ball he was too proud to dodge. He was the only major Indian leader to lose his life in battles with white troops during the uprising. The chief's body was taken from the battlefield, as was customary among the Sioux.* PHOTO TAKEN IN 1858.

WILLIAM R. MARSHALL, *who was lieutenant colonel of the Seventh Minnesota in 1862, went on to become a general in the Civil War. Later he served as Minnesota's fifth governor.* PHOTO BY CHARLES A. ZIMMERMAN, ST. PAUL, 1864.

in the Civil War, had been surrendered by their commander at Murfreesboro, Tennessee, on July 13, and had been paroled. The Third's officers, however, were still Confederate prisoners, and the regiment was commanded by Major Abraham E. Welch of the Fourth Minnesota.

Sibley expected that the addition of these well-drilled troops would inspire confidence in his other regiments and add to the effectiveness of his command. Once more he laid plans to march. Again he was delayed—this time by two days of heavy rain that turned the prairie trails into muddy bogs. Finally, on September 19 Sibley left Fort Ridgely to begin his march up the valley. Besides the men of the Third Minnesota, his army consisted of nine companies of the Sixth regiment, five companies of the Seventh under Lieutenant Colonel William R. Marshall (a future Civil War hero and state governor), a company of the Ninth Minnesota, thirty-eight Renville Rangers, twenty-eight mounted citizen guards, and some sixteen citizen-artillerists—in all 1,619 men. Reverend Riggs, the veteran missionary, went along as chaplain and interpreter, and Other Day acted as a scout.

Four days of easy marching along the government road to the Upper Agency found Sibley's troops encamped on the night of September 22 on the east shore of Lone Tree or Battle Lake (which has since dried up) about five miles north of present-day Echo. The guide mistook this small body of water for Wood Lake (actually located three and a half miles to the west), and thus the battle that ensued is incorrectly named.

The outlet of Lone Tree Lake was a small stream that curved northeastward through a deepening ravine and then wound to the east. The Sixth Minnesota camped to the left on the lake front. Next on the right, the Third held the crest of the southern slope of the ravine, while the Seventh was located to the right rear behind the ravine. Thus a roughly triangular line was formed.

Thinking that the Indians were farther up the valley, Sibley failed to station pickets very far outside the camp. Actually, from 700 to 1,200 Dakota braves that night stole down from their camp near the Chippewa River and held a council only a few miles from Sibley's encampment. Little Crow considered launching a night attack on the troops, but decided instead to ambush the soldiers next morning when they were strung out along the road. Dawn the following day found the Indians hiding quietly in the tall grass waiting for the troops to break camp.

Fortunately for Sibley and his men, the Third Minnesota lacked the discipline it once had and would soon have again. Several men of that regiment apparently decided they would supplement their rations with potatoes from the gardens at the Upper Agency, some three miles to the north. About 7:00 A.M. they hitched up wagons and took off, seemingly without permission. "They came on over the prairie," said Big Eagle, "right where part of our [*the Indian*] line was. Some of the wagons were not in the road, and if they had kept straight on would have driven right over our men as they lay in the grass. At last they came so close that our men had to rise up and fire." Several soldiers were wounded; the others jumped from the wagons and returned the fire. Back at camp, other men of the Third grabbed their guns and advanced without orders to aid their comrades.

THIS VIEW *of a creek in the area where the battle of Wood Lake was fought shows the rolling prairie country as it looks today.* PHOTO BY BECKER.

At first the Indians gave way before the small advancing battalion. Then they gathered their forces and deployed in their usual fan-shaped fashion to threaten the army's flank. Seeing the danger, Sibley ordered the Third back, but he had to issue the order twice before the men obeyed. Welch was wounded, and Lieutenant Rollin C. Olin took command.

Meanwhile Sibley noticed Indians moving toward the ravine on the right and ordered Marshall to that sector of the field. Captain Mark Hendricks swept the ravine with canister from his six-pounder, and Marshall then cleared the area with five companies of the Seventh and one of the Sixth. Another company of the Sixth under Major Robert N. McLaren repelled a threatened advance near the lake.

The Indians withdrew unpursued after about two hours of fighting. One of the casualties in the battle was Chief Mankato, who is said to have been killed by a cannon ball he refused to dodge. His body was carried away, but those of fourteen other Indians remained on the field. Some of these were scalped by the soldiers. Learning this, Sibley expressed his stern disapproval and promised severe punishment to any men who repeated such treatment. "The bodies of the dead," he said, "even of a savage enemy shall not be subjected to indignities by civilized & christian men."

The battle of Wood Lake was a decisive victory for Sibley's forces, although seven soldiers were killed and thirty-three wounded. Writing to his wife after the fight on September 23, Sibley said that the Indians had received "a severe blow" and "will not dare to make another stand." He was right. The battle of Wood Lake marked the end of organized warfare by the Sioux in Minnesota, and it pointed the way for the release of the captives and the capture of many of the Indians.

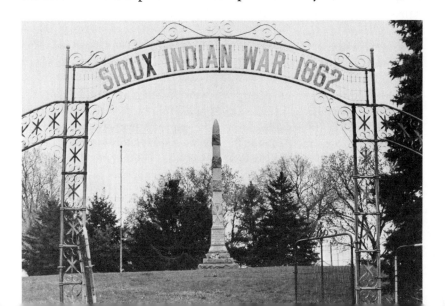

WOOD LAKE STATE MONUMENT *on the site of the battle names the seven soldiers killed there. The granite shaft and neat little park are located just west of Highway 67 between Echo and Granite Falls.* PHOTO BY CARLEY.

13.
SURRENDER AT CAMP RELEASE

CAMP RELEASE, *made up of the tents and wagons of the soldiers, was located near present-day Montevideo.* FROM HEARD, *Sioux War.*

COLONEL SIBLEY decided to remain at the Lone Tree Lake camp for two days to care for the wounded and work out his strategy. He realized that from a military point of view he should have gone after the retreating Indians, but he lacked the cavalry to make a vigorous pursuit. (With sufficient cavalry, Sibley might have been able to capture many of the Sioux leaders, thereby eliminating the need for the later punitive expeditions into Dakota Territory.) Moreover, he feared that chasing the hostiles might inspire them to murder the white and mixed-blood captives they held. There is evidence that Little Crow and others did threaten to kill the prisoners after returning from the Wood Lake battlefield. By then, however, Little Crow had lost much of his influence, and the warriors did not carry out the threat.

There was good reason for Sibley to believe that the battle at Wood Lake had widened the split in the Sioux ranks and swelled the number who wanted to make peace. In addition to Chiefs Wabasha and Taopi, other Indians had for some time been trying to end the hostilities. The Wahpeton orator, Little Paul, especially, had spoken out boldly in more than one council for releasing the prisoners and ending the war. Many Christian Indians and other "friendlies" had been protecting the whites brought into the Indian camps.

TAOPI (*Wounded Man*), *a friendly Mdewakanton chief, joined Wabasha in arranging for the safe release of the white and mixed-blood prisoners.* PHOTO BY MARTIN'S GALLERY, ST. PAUL, 1862.

Before the Wood Lake battle, the Lower Sioux had moved steadily up the Minnesota Valley until they were stopped by Red Iron, a Wahpeton chief, whose village was across the river from present-day Montevideo. Backed by Chief Standing Buffalo, a Sisseton, and other Upper Sioux who wanted no part in the hostilities, Red Iron threatened to fire on Little Crow's followers if they set foot into his territory. After several instances of near-fighting between the two factions, Red Iron and other Indians and mixed-bloods friendly to the whites moved to a new camp a short distance from the mouth of the Chippewa. The Sioux who wished to continue the war set up their tepees about a half mile to the west.

While Little Crow and his braves were fighting at Wood Lake, the friendlies took control of the captives and brought them into their own camp. They dug rifle pits to defend the captives in the expected fight with Little Crow's men should they come back victorious from battle. But when these forces returned defeated, the prisoners and the growing number of friendlies watched the Sioux leader as well as Chiefs Shakopee, Red Middle Voice, Medicine Bottle, and others hastily

64

gather their families and belongings and head for the open prairie beyond easy reach of the soldiers.

Those in charge of the friendly camp—Wabasha, Red Iron, Taopi, the influential mixed-blood Gabriel Renville, and others — then sent Joseph Campbell, a mixed-blood prisoner, to let Sibley know that the captives were safe and the soldiers could come up. The troops left Lone Tree Lake on September 25 and made a leisurely march of about ten miles to Riggs's deserted Hazelwood mission. There the soldiers held a dress parade to impress upon any undecided Indians the need for surrender. Perhaps the exercise was also calculated to raise the soldiers' morale.

About noon the next day, Sibley moved up and encamped his army a short distance north of the tents where the captives were held. Besides the prisoners, the 150 lodges of the Indian camp were occupied by Mdewakanton under Wabasha and Taopi, who had never favored the war, other Lower Sioux now tired of the conflict and ready to take their chances on surrender, many Wahpeton (including mixed-bloods), and a few Sisseton. Because it never was known which was the dominant group, the Upper and Lower Sioux quarreled for years afterward about which should get credit for rescuing the captives.

Sibley, unmounted but with an escort of troops, entered the Indian camp "with drums beating and colors flying" at about two o'clock on the afternoon of September 26. In a report to General Pope the next day, the colonel wrote of the event: "The Indians and half-breeds assembled . . . in considerable numbers, and I proceeded to give them very briefly my views of the late proceedings; my determination that the guilty parties should be pursued and overtaken, if possible, and I made a demand that all the captives should be delivered to me instantly, that I might take them to my camp."

The friendlies at once released 91 whites and about 150 mixed-bloods. Additional captives, freed in the next few days, brought the total to 107 whites and 162 mixed-bloods — 269 in all. Most of the whites rescued were women and children, there being not more than four men (some historians say George Spencer was the only one). Among

RED IRON (above), an Upper Sioux chief who stood up to Little Crow to ensure the prisoners' safety, greeted Sibley as the commander entered the Indian camp (left). The painting incorrectly shows the men mounted. With others, Red Iron had set up the captives' camp opposite the mouth of the Chippewa River. SCENE (LEFT) FROM STEVENS PANORAMA; PHOTO (ABOVE) BY WHITNEY, 1862, AFTER ONE TAKEN IN NEW YORK CITY, 1858.

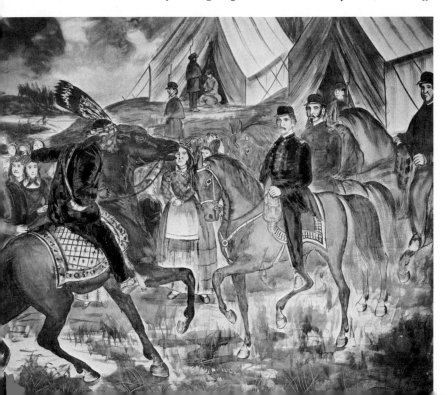

those rescued were Mrs. Brown and her family, Mrs. Wakefield (who was openly critical of Sibley's slowness), Mary Schwandt, Mattie Williams, Mrs. Amos Huggins, and Nancy M. Faribault and her mixed-blood husband, David. The grateful captives were taken to Camp Release, as Sibley's encampment was called, where some of the soldiers gave their clothes to the needy women.

Describing the liberation, Isaac V. D. Heard, an eyewitness, later wrote: "The poor creatures wept for joy at their escape. They had watched for our coming for many a weary day, with constant apprehensions of death at the hands of their savage captors, and had almost despaired of seeing us. The woe written in the faces of the half starved and nearly naked women and children would have melted the hardest heart." This description was doubtless applicable to most of the released captives, but Sibley wrote his wife about a couple of exceptions. He said that a Mrs. Harriet Adams, "whose six months old child was killed when she was captured" and "who is exceedingly pretty," told him she was let alone and protected by a friendly Indian, who treated her like a sister. (In a reminiscence several years later, Mary Schwandt expressed annoyance over Mrs. Adams' seeming contentment with her lot.) Sibley also said that a second unidentified "rather handsome" captive "had become so infatuated with the redskin who had taken her for a wife that, although her white husband was still living . . . and had been in search of her, she declared that were it not for her children, she would not leave her dusky paramour."

Both before and after the events at Camp Release, Sibley's men had a hand in rescuing (or at least welcoming) fugitives from the Indians. The expedition was at the point of leaving Fort Ridgely when the men saw a Christian Indian named Lorenzo Lawrence arriving on the river below with his family and Mrs. Joseph W. De Camp, wife of the government sawmill operator at the Lower Sioux Agency, and her three children. Lawrence had helped the De Camps escape from the Sioux, who had captured them at the agency during the attack of August 18. The party, with very little food, had made its way downriver from near the mouth of the Chippewa in leaky boats and rainy weather. At the fort Mrs. De Camp learned to her sorrow that her husband, who was in St. Paul on business when his wife and children were captured, had returned to look for them and had been mortally wounded at Birch Coulee. She later married the Reverend Joshua Sweet, the chaplain at Fort Ridgely who attended De Camp before his death.

In late October a foraging party of Sibley's men came upon an emaciated woman and her three-year-old daughter near starvation on the north side of the Minnesota River near the Upper Agency. The woman was Mrs. Justina Boelter, whose husband John had been killed with his parents and other relatives on the family's farm near Beaver Creek on August 18. For some nine weeks, Mrs. Boelter and her daughter, Ottilie, had survived in the woods without fire or shelter. They had eaten raw potatoes and grape leaves to stay alive. A second daughter, Amelia, who was about five years old, had died of starvation on September 24. By then the mother was so weak she could not help her. The rescuing soldiers wept at the sight, but Ottilie and Mrs. Boelter both eventually regained their health. The latter later married her brother-

CAMP RELEASE STATE MONUMENT *marks the site where the captives were freed on September 26, 1862. The imposing fifty-one-foot shaft stands on a knoll about two miles west of Montevideo.* PHOTO BY BECKER.

66

in-law, Michael Boelter, who had lost his wife and three daughters in the August 18 attack.

On September 23 Sibley sent some of the released captives to Fort Ridgely; orphaned children were sent to the settlements beyond. Several of the women remained at Camp Release to testify at the trials of Indians who would soon appear before the military commission set up by Sibley to punish the hostile Sioux.

From Camp Release, Sibley wrote Pope asking to be relieved of his command. He felt that the two objectives of his expedition — defeating the Indians and delivering their prisoners — had been accomplished, and he thought "a strictly military commander" would be better fitted for the task of exterminating those Indians who had escaped. Sibley's request was not granted, and on September 29 the president recommended his promotion to brigadier general of volunteers, although Congressional approval of his appointment was long delayed.

When the army took over the friendly camp, about 1,200 Indians were taken into custody. This number increased daily as individuals and small parties of Sioux, many of them facing starvation, continued to surrender under flags of truce. As they came in, they were put into a separate camp nearby. The number of Sioux thus captured eventually totaled nearly two thousand. Feeding the Indians as well as his own men was a critical problem for Sibley; thus, on October 4 he sent 1,250 Sioux under guard to gather corn and potatoes from the fields about the ruined Upper Agency. While parties of soldiers scoured the region for more captives, the mass trial of Indians who had taken part in the uprising got under way at Sibley's Camp Release headquarters.

THE JOYOUS LIBERATION *of 269 whites and mixed-bloods at Camp Release is depicted below. Most of the captives had roamed about with the Indians for five weeks, fearing from day to day that they would be killed.* SCENE FROM GAG-HELLER-SCHWENDINGER PANORAMA.

14.
PUNISHMENT
OF THE SIOUX

CONDEMNED SIOUX PRISONERS *awaited their fate in a crowded prison at Mankato.* DRAWING BY W. H. CHILDS FROM *Frank Leslie's Illustrated Newspaper,* JANUARY 31, 1863.

THE FIVE-MAN military commission appointed to try the Sioux who participated in the outbreak first convened at Camp Release on September 28. Some weeks later, Sibley moved his army and its Indian prisoners to the Lower Agency, where the trials were resumed on October 25. Members of the commission were Colonel William Crooks, Lieutenant Colonel Marshall, who was soon replaced by Major George Bradley of the Seventh regiment, Captains Hiram P. Grant and Hiram S. Bailey, and Lieutenant Rollin C. Olin, who served as judge advocate. Olin was assisted by Isaac Heard, a St. Paul lawyer and early historian of the uprising, who acted as recorder.

The commissioners also had the help of Antoine D. Frenière, a mixed-blood, and the Reverend Riggs as interpreters. The latter gathered much of the evidence used to identify and arraign the prisoners, although he later denied serving as a virtual "Grand Jury," as Heard claimed. Many of the cases were expedited, and many prisoners convicted, by the testimony of Joseph Godfrey (or Otakle), a mulatto born of a Black mother and a French-Canadian father. Godfrey was married to a Dakota woman and had lived at the Lower Agency for five years. He was the first prisoner to be tried, was found guilty of murder, and was sentenced "to be hung by the neck until he is dead." Although the evidence in the trial transcripts appears more convincing in Godfrey's case than in many others, the commission decided to commute his sentence to ten years in prison after he turned state's evidence. He proved to be an intelligent, articulate witness who rebutted in detail the testimony of a number of his late colleagues in the war. Afterward, Godfrey served three of the ten years of his prison sentence. He was then released, along with others, to live with the Dakota at Niobrara, Nebraska. There he farmed industriously until his death in 1909.

68

Although the commissioners began their task deliberately and with the intention of dispensing reasonable justice, they soon found that there were many more prisoners to be tried than had been anticipated. Twenty-nine cases had been disposed of by October 4 at Camp Release. Two weeks later the number tried had mounted to more than 120, but nearly 300 more cases still remained on the docket and Pope was pushing Sibley to complete the job. After the trials resumed at the Lower Sioux Agency in François La Bathe's log house that had escaped fire on August 18, the pace was stepped up so that the remaining cases were disposed of in ten days. The commission settled up to forty cases in a single day; some were heard in as little as five minutes. When it finished its work on November 5, the commission had tried 392 prisoners, sentenced 307 to death, and given 16 prison terms. Sibley promptly approved all except one case and passed the results on to Pope. The one case was that of John Other Day's brother, whose death sentence Sibley remitted to imprisonment for lack of conclusive evidence and because of Other Day's earnest appeal.

Reading the records today buttresses the impression that the trials were a travesty of justice. It is true that those in charge had to resist public pressure to do away with all the Indians, guilty and innocent alike, and it must also be pointed out that the trials were conducted by a military commission and not by a court of law. Nevertheless, many of the proceedings were too hasty and quite a number of prisoners were condemned on flimsy evidence. Many Indians who had expected to be treated as prisoners of war were sentenced to death merely for being present at such battles as New Ulm and Birch Coulee. As soon as a prisoner admitted firing a shot at whites, no matter where, the commission with unseemly haste sentenced him to hang.

The unsophisticated Indians were caught up, too, in proceedings they did not understand. They would readily admit an act — like fighting

THE LOG HOUSE *of François La Bathe at the Lower Agency was the rude "courtroom" where many of the Sioux trials were held. Soldiers are shown guarding the Indian prisoners.* PHOTO BY WHITNEY, *1862.*

in a battle — that would condemn them, and then offer what the whites regarded as often ludicrous extenuating circumstances. Perhaps two-thirds of the prisoners admitted firing one, two, or three shots, which they maintained seldom hit anyone. Their aim, they said, was always bad. Others claimed to be roasting and eating corn and beef behind the scenes while fighting was going on. Others could not participate because they suffered from bellyaches (maybe from the corn) or sore eyes. One said that a horse he had stolen was only a very little one, and another reported that he took a pair of oxen for his wife. Several who confessed offered as a defense the fact that they were church members. And quite a number testified that they were cowards and therefore afraid to join the battles.

Both Sibley and Pope favored the immediate execution of the condemned Indians, but each doubted that his authority extended "quite so far," as Sibley put it. Consequently, the question of who had the authority to order the execution of the Sioux was passed to President Lincoln for consideration in mid-October. The list of condemned was cut to 303 Indians and mixed-bloods, whose names Pope on November 7 telegraphed to the president at a cost of four hundred dollars. Lincoln then asked Pope to forward "the full and complete record of their convictions . . . by mail." When the papers arrived, Lincoln put two men to work studying them. He wanted to make a distinction between rapists and wanton murderers on the one hand and Indians who merely participated in battles on the other.

While the president's representatives reviewed the trial records, Sibley transferred the uncondemned Sioux who had surrendered — about 1,700 men, women, and children — to Fort Snelling, where it would be easier for the government to feed them. On November 7, the Indians set out on the long trek from the Lower Agency to the fort. The procession was four miles long. As the bedraggled Sioux passed through Henderson, white citizens, incensed at the sight of their hated enemies, attacked the prisoners with knives, guns, clubs, and stones. Many Indians were maltreated before the soldiers guarding them succeeded in subduing their attackers. Reaching Fort Snelling on November 13, the captives were placed in a gloomy, fenced camp of tepees on the north bank of the Minnesota River. There they spent a wretched winter awaiting the government's decision regarding their future.

The 303 Indians who had been condemned to death were moved by Sibley and his troops on November 9 from the Lower Agency to Camp Lincoln at South Bend. At New Ulm, enraged citizens, many of whom were reburying their dead at the time, violently attacked the captives. Writing to his wife, Sibley said that the Indians were "set upon by a crowd of men[,] women, and children, who showered brickbats and other missiles upon the shackled wretches." Fifteen Indians and some of the guards were severely injured. It took a bayonet charge by Sibley's men to drive the whites back.

During the night of December 4 an army of citizens from Mankato marched toward Camp Lincoln, intent on murdering the Indians. They were stopped by the troops. The following day the Indians were moved to safer quarters in a log structure at Mankato.

Soon after establishing the condemned prisoners in Camp Lincoln, Sibley turned his command over to Colonel Stephen A. Miller of the Seventh Minnesota. On November 25 Sibley became head of a new Military District of Minnesota, created by the war department with headquarters at St. Paul.

Meanwhile President Lincoln was being bombarded with appeals from the press, Governor Ramsey, General Pope, and many others. They urged the immediate execution of the entire list of convicted Indians. Only one really effective voice from Minnesota was raised in protest — that of Bishop Whipple. The clergyman had visited Lincoln shortly after the fighting ended. At that time, said the president, Whipple "talked with me about the rascality of this Indian business until I felt it down to my boots." On December 17, 1862, Whipple asked "What Shall We Do with the Indians?" in a letter to the *St. Paul Pioneer.* The question "is not to be settled by passion," he wrote, "but by calm thought, as becomes men who meet duties in the fear of God. History will strip off every flimsy pretext, and lay bare the folly of every shallow expedient." Riggs and Dr. Williamson also wrote unpopular letters to the press calling for a fair trial for the Indians.

On December 6, 1862, Lincoln disappointed most Minnesotans by approving death sentences for only 39 of the 303 convicts. He wrote out the names of those to be hanged for rape and murder and set the day of their execution as December 19, 1862. Later he permitted a week's postponement to allow more time for arrangements.

Colonel Miller informed the Indians of Lincoln's decision. To Major Brown fell the task of identifying those on the president's list—an awesome responsibility since several had identical or very similar names. The thirty-nine condemned Sioux were then separated from the rest of the prisoners and securely chained.

Throughout the week preceding the execution, the missionaries—Williamson, Riggs, Father Augustin Ravoux, and others—spent a great deal of time with the convicts. Most of the thirty-nine were baptized, including Tatemima (or Round Wind), who was reprieved at the last minute because he had been convicted on the testimony of two young boys. On Christmas and the day before, relatives were allowed to visit the doomed men to say good-by and receive mementos. Several of the prisoners broke down during these last interviews, while others, in the Dakota tradition, faced death stoically.

The eloquent Rdainyanka, whose speech in support of continuing the war was quoted earlier, dictated a letter to his father-in-law, Wabasha. His bitter, tragic words may have reflected the real feelings of others: "You have deceived me," the young man said. "You told me that if we followed the advice of General Sibley, and give ourselves up to the whites, all would be well; no innocent man would be injured. I have not killed, wounded, or injured a white man, or any white persons. I have not participated in the plunder of their property; and yet to-day I am set apart for execution, and must die in a few days, while men who are guilty will remain in prison. My wife is your daughter, my children are your grandchildren. I leave them all in your care and under your protection. Do not let them suffer; and when my children

are grown up, let them know that their father died because he followed the advice of his chief, and without having the blood of a white man to answer for to the Great Spirit.

"My wife and children are dear to me. Let them not grieve for me. Let them remember that the brave should be prepared to meet death; and I will do as becomes a Dakota."

THE NAMES of the thirty-nine Sioux to be executed at Mankato were carefully written by President Lincoln himself on executive mansion stationery. The first and last pages of the three-page manuscript are reproduced here. The document was presented to the Minnesota Historical Society in 1868 by Edward D. Neill, a Minnesota clergyman who was one of Lincoln's secretaries.

The Indians began chanting their death songs early on the morning of December 26. They continued this ritual while Brown and his assistants prepared them for the gallows, which had been built in the Mankato public square. Their chains were removed, and their arms were bound with cords. The dirge ceased as the soldiers placed on each doomed head a white cap, which would be rolled down over each face before the execution. The Indians objected to these caps, regarding them as a great humiliation. All crouched in silence, some listening to Father Ravoux, and some painting their faces.

At 10:00 A.M., the thirty-eight prisoners marched from the prison to the wooden scaffold, which was surrounded by solid ranks of more than 1,400 soldiers on hand to keep order. Many curious citizens

LAST-MINUTE LIKENESSES *of some of the condemned Dakota were made the morning of their final day on earth by Robert O. Sweeny, a St. Paul artist. Five of them are shown on this page, along with a sketch (upper left) of the mulatto Godfrey whose sentence was commuted for turning state's evidence.* INK WASH DRAWINGS BY SWEENY, 1862.

JOSEPH GODFREY

RED LEAF

WHITE DOG

RDAINYANKA

MAKATANAJIN

BAPTISTE CAMPBELL

74

crowded the streets for a glimpse of the condemned, and more on-lookers stared from roof tops and windows. Once more the "Hi-yi-yi" of the Sioux death song began as the prisoners mounted the gallows and the caps were drawn over their faces. Major Brown began a slow, measured drumbeat. At the third roll, William Duley, a survivor of the Lake Shetek murders, stepped forward and cut the rope. "As the platform fell, there was one, not loud, but prolonged cheer from the soldiery and citizens . . . and then all were quiet and earnest." Thus an eyewitness described the event that has been called "America's greatest mass execution."

The dead were buried in a single shallow grave near the river front. That night several doctors, quick to seize the rare opportunity to obtain subjects for anatomical study, dug up the bodies. Dr. William Mayo drew that of Cut Nose, and later his sons learned osteology from the Indian's skeleton.

Two notorious participants in the uprising of 1862 — Chiefs Shakopee and Medicine Bottle — later figured in a plot that brought about their capture in Canada under questionable circumstances. Conspirators on the Canadian side of the border got the Indians drunk in the spring of 1864, drugged and bound them, and delivered them to Major Edwin A. C. Hatch of St. Paul, who was waiting with his independent battalion of cavalry at Pembina on the American side. The hapless Indian leaders were taken to Fort Snelling and sentenced to death on rather flimsy evidence. The execution took place there on November 11, 1865. Legend has it that Shakopee heard one of the state's early steam locomotives as he mounted the gallows. Pointing to the train, he is said to have exclaimed: "As the white man comes in the Indian goes out."

75

15.

BANISHMENT
FROM
MINNESOTA

MOST MINNESOTANS were so enraged over the Indian war that they were not satisfied even by the mass hanging of thirty-eight Sioux. They demanded that the Indians who had escaped to roam the prairies of Dakota Territory be pursued and punished and that all the captured Sioux be banished from the state — the 1,700 or so peaceful Indians, mostly women and children, confined near Fort Snelling as well as the 300 or more men imprisoned at Mankato who had been convicted by the commission but not executed.

Incited by a resentful press, white Minnesotans were not disposed to distinguish between hostile and friendly Indians. A further indication of this unreasoning attitude was the concerted effort to remove the peaceful Winnebago Indians from their reservation in Blue Earth County to some place beyond the state's borders. The Winnebago had taken little or no part in the Sioux War and had already suffered several removals in the past. The fact that they lived on choice farm lands coveted by the whites raises a presumption that the settlers may well have been prompted by economic motives, coupled with fear and prejudice, in wanting to get rid of the unfortunate Winnebago.

Political leaders echoed (and at times fanned) demands for Indian removal. As early as September 9, 1862, Governor Ramsey had declared that "The Sioux Indians of Minnesota must be exterminated or driven forever beyond the borders of the State." He also called for abrogating all Sioux treaties and using annuity money due the Indians to reimburse white victims of the Dakota War. Congress eventually accepted this suggestion, appropriating $200,000 in an act passed on February 16, 1863, and an additional $1,170,374 in 1864. A commission was set up to distribute Indian money for claims, many of which were criticized for being extravagant. Thousands of dollars, for example, were claimed for damage to rutabagas in the fields. One factor among many difficult to assess was the extent of damage done to abandoned farms by plundering white men and women for which the Indians received the blame.

But many people in the 1860s were more concerned about Indian relocation than about depredations. On December 16, 1862, Minnesota Senator Morton S. Wilkinson and Congressman William Windom introduced bills for the removal of both the Sioux and the Winnebago. The Winnebago act became law on February 21, 1863, and the Sioux act on March 3. Worded in general terms, the acts specified that the Indians were to be relocated on unoccupied land "well adapted for agricultural purposes" but beyond the limits of any state and that money derived from the sale of their old reservation lands should be invested for the tribes' benefit.

Congress appropriated only about $50,000 to transfer the Sioux and a like amount for the Winnebago. Acting for the president, Dole, commissioner of Indian affairs, and John P. Usher, new secretary of the interior, decided to locate both tribes on the Missouri River within a hundred miles of Fort Randall in Dakota Territory. This site could be supplied by river and would permit the Fort Randall garrison to guard and contain the Indians. Specific arrangements were left to Clark W. Thompson, superintendent of Indian affairs for the northern district, which included Minnesota. Like Agent Galbraith before him, Thompson was a Republican political appointee.

When navigation opened on the Mississippi River in the spring of 1863, the first Dakota people to be transported from Minnesota were the prisoners at Mankato. During the winter the prison was "one great school," said missionary Riggs, because he and the convicts who had attended mission schools helped the other prisoners learn to read and write in their own language. The prison also was an active church; Dr. Williamson and others conducted frequent services and prayer meetings. Lacking access to their medicine men, the Sioux became praying and hymn-singing Christians. Missionaries Williamson and Gideon H. Pond baptized more than 300 prisoners, 274 of them on one day, February 3, 1863.

Fearful of possible mob violence, Commissioner Dole tried to keep secret the arrangements for the prisoners' transfer from Mankato to military barracks at Camp McClellan near Davenport, Iowa. Although Mankatoans knew by mid-April that the prisoners would be leaving soon, they were not aware of the exact departure date until April 21,

THIS MAP shows where the various splinters of the Dakota people settled or were imprisoned after the 1862 uprising. MAP BY ALAN OMINSKY.

when the steamboat "Favorite" docked on its return from an upriver trip to Fort Ridgely. The next morning, soldiers of the Seventh Minnesota Regiment kept the crowd away by forming two lines through which the Sioux could pass unmolested from the log prison to the boat. Fifteen to twenty women who had been cooks and housekeepers for the prisoners boarded first, followed by forty-eight men who had been acquitted of formal charges, and then by the convicts chained in pairs. A military escort of eighty-five men from the Seventh regiment's Company C accompanied them. The Indians sang hymns and conducted devotional services as the "Favorite" made its way down the Minnesota River to Fort Snelling, where most of the women and all of the forty-eight acquitted men were hurriedly put ashore to join the uncomfortable camp of the 1,700 Sioux who had been there all winter. The boat took the others down the Mississippi to a prison at Davenport without further incident.

The prisoners were confined at Davenport for three years, much of the time under the guidance of Dr. Williamson. At his urging some forty of them were pardoned in 1864. At last in April, 1866, after about 120 had died in prison, the remaining 247 were pardoned by President Andrew Johnson. The following June they were finally allowed to rejoin their families, who were then living on the Santee Reservation near Niobrara, Nebraska.

Meanwhile, Superintendent Thompson had arranged with Pierre Chouteau, Jr., and Company of St. Louis to transport the Sioux being held at Fort Snelling as well as the Winnebago in Blue Earth County to their Dakota Territory destinations for twenty-five dollars a head and subsistence at ten cents each per day. Like the Sioux imprisoned at Mankato, the larger body at Fort Snelling had experienced a widespread revival of learning and religion during the winter. Working

IN THIS DISMAL FENCED ENCLOSURE *on the Minnesota River below Fort Snelling, the uncondemned Sioux prisoners spent a miserable winter in 1862–63. Many died, and many became Christians.* PHOTO BY B. F. UPTON, 1862.

among them were such missionaries as Father Ravoux, Samuel Hinman (who had served at the Lower Sioux Agency and escaped), and, most notably, John Poage Williamson, the eldest son of Dr. Williamson. The younger Williamson had spoken the Dakota language since childhood, had begun building a church in 1862 when the uprising interrupted his work, and had rejoined the Dakota when they were sent to Fort Snelling. He was to spend the rest of his life as a missionary among them.

Quite a few Sioux captives died during the winter and early spring in the cold, inadequate encampment near Fort Snelling. For those who remained, concern about their fate added to their frustration. A bleak picture began to unfold for them in early May, 1863, when the Indian office "prepared to ship them off like so many cattle," as historian Folwell put it. Immediate arrangements were in the hands of special agent Benjamin Thompson, brother of the superintendent. To be deported were slightly more than 1,300, of whom only about 125 were men capable of bearing arms. On May 4 some 770 Indians, accompanied by the Reverend Hinman and forty men of Company G of the Tenth Minnesota as an escort, boarded the river steamer "Davenport," which was only 35 feet wide and 205 feet long, for the trip down the Mississippi to St. Louis.

During a half-hour stop at St. Paul for the steamer to take on cargo, several Indian women on the boiler deck were injured, some severely, by stones thrown by an ugly mob that gathered at the levee. The escorting soldiers had to threaten a bayonet charge to stop the "gross outrage," as the *St. Paul Weekly Press* called it. The "Davenport" reached St. Louis on May 8. Its crowded passengers were then transferred to the steamer "Florence," and on May 9 the Dakota started their long voyage up the Missouri River.

On May 5 a second "cargo" of 547 Sioux at Fort Snelling, accompanied by John Williamson and Benjamin Thompson, boarded the steamboat "Northerner" for an uneventful trip down the Mississippi to Hannibal, Missouri. There they were herded into railroad freight cars, sixty to a car, and taken overland to St. Joseph on the Missouri River. When the "Florence," already "swarming with Sioux Indians," landed at St. Joseph, the second group was also jammed on board. For the remaining eight-hundred-mile trip up the shallow, tortuous Missouri, the steamer was horribly crowded with 1,300 Indians, many of whom got sick drinking filthy water and eating musty hardtack and briny pork.

The exact destination of the Sioux had been fixed only a short time earlier by Superintendent Thompson, who had made a hurried reconnaissance and decided upon a reservation near the mouth of Crow Creek on the east bank of the Missouri about 150 miles above Fort Randall in what is now southeastern South Dakota. This turned out to be a dismal, drought-stricken place that was soon dotted by Sioux graves.

And what of the Winnebago Indians in Blue Earth County? Their agent, another political appointee named St. Andre Durand Balcombe, had the unpleasant task of informing them that they would be moved to the Missouri River. By May 9 about a thousand had been reluctantly congregated at Camp Porter in Mankato, where they held scalp dances in protest. Before arriving, some members of Little Priest's band had

JOHN P. WILLIAMSON *grew up among the Sioux as the eldest son of veteran missionary Thomas S. Williamson. He became a missionary in 1860 and rejoined the Sioux at Fort Snelling after the uprising. He accompanied them to Dakota Territory and spent the rest of his life among them. His wife Sarah (below) assisted him for many years. They are shown at the time of their marriage in 1866 near Winnebago City, Minnesota.* PHOTOS FROM WINIFRED W. BARTON, *John P. Williamson: A Brother to the Sioux* (NEW YORK, 1919).

killed and scalped two Sioux, perhaps in the hope of winning favor with the whites and, more certainly, because they blamed the Sioux for their troubles. This act was later to create considerable tension.

On May 9 and 10 three river packets took about 1,200 Winnebago down the Minnesota to Fort Snelling. From there they were transported down the Mississippi on the "Canada" and the "Davenport" to Hannibal. Like the Sioux, they then rode railroad cars to St. Joseph and, after a similarly slow voyage up the Missouri, arrived at Crow Creek on June 8 aboard the regular packet "West Wind."

About 750 Winnebago followers of old Chief Winneshiek at first refused to leave Blue Earth County. Then they succumbed to a military threat and were transported separately to Crow Creek. When they arrived on June 24, the transfer of 1,300 Sioux and nearly 1,950 Winnebago was completed.

Before long, fifty workmen hired by Superintendent Thompson constructed agency buildings at Crow Creek and enclosed them within a 400-square-foot wooden stockade that was placed near the dividing line of the adjacent Sioux and Winnebago reservations. The stockaded post was at first named Usher's Landing for the secretary of the interior, but soon it became known as Fort Thompson.

Both the Sioux and the Winnebago hated their new homes. They also feared each other. The Sioux had been alarmed by the Winnebago scalping of two of their number at Mankato, and the Winnebago were afraid of raids by hostile Sioux roaming the prairies. Within a short time many Winnebago went southward to the Omaha Reservation in Nebraska, where, by a later treaty, they were allowed to remain.

The Sioux at Crow Creek, unable to grow crops as the government

THE "DAVENPORT" *was one of the Mississippi River packets that transported the Dakota Indians "like cattle" from their encampment near Fort Snelling in 1863 to St. Louis. From there they were moved by other steamboats up the Missouri to Crow Creek in Dakota Territory.*

had hoped, saw their numbers dwindle for lack of proper nourishment, clothing, and shelter. Aware that he would have to supply food or the Indians would starve, Superintendent Thompson contracted to have pork, flour, and beef cattle moved overland from Mankato late in 1863 in what was sarcastically dubbed the "Moscow Expedition." The pork and flour that arrived was condemned as unfit for soldiers to eat, and the three hundred head of cattle became emaciated on the three hundred-mile trek to the reservation. Nevertheless, the flour and meat, including entrails and other undesirable parts, were the main ingredients of a nauseous stew that was cooked in vats and ladeled out to the Indian women. The "rotten stuff" was understandably refused by many Dakota. The younger Williamson helped to organize a buffalo hunt that supplemented the Indians' diet during the first winter, but it was soon obvious that Crow Creek was not a suitable site for an agricultural reservation. After three distressful years there, the Sioux were removed to the Santee Reservation near the mouth of the Niobrara River in Nebraska. There life gradually improved for them.

Space does not permit a detailed account of all the fragmented Sioux scattered by the holocaust of the 1862 uprising, but a few should be mentioned. When the Indians at Fort Snelling departed in the spring of 1863, between one hundred and two hundred Lower Sioux "friendlies" were allowed to remain. Many of these became scouts for Sibley's army during the 1863 campaign in Dakota Territory. With their families, they settled near Big Stone Lake. Others of this group became impoverished wanderers or settled near Faribault and Mendota on the private lands of Alexander Faribault and Sibley. Largely because of the efforts of Bishop Whipple, Congress on February 9, 1865, appropriated $7,500 "for the relief of certain friendly Indians of the Sioux nation, in Minnesota." One third of this amount (which Whipple thought was too much) was to go to John Other Day for his help in rescuing sixty-two persons from the Upper Agency during the war.

After five years of roaming the plains west of Minnesota, the Upper Sioux (Sisseton and Wahpeton) were gathered in 1867 on reservations at Devils Lake in North Dakota and at Sisseton in South Dakota. Head

chief of both bands from 1884 (when Chief Red Iron died) until his death in 1892 was Gabriel Renville, the nephew of Lac qui Parle trader Joseph Renville and a relative by marriage of Joseph R. Brown. These reservations have been the home, albeit often a poor one, of many Minnesota Upper Sioux and their descendants from that day to this. Unfortunately, the system of allotting land to individual members of the tribe, introduced by the government in 1887, served to reduce the size of these reservations, as it did many others.

As early as the late 1860s small groups of Dakota began returning to Minnesota. They settled in places like Prairie Island in the Mississippi River upstream from Red Wing, at Prior Lake, and at their old homes near the Upper and Lower agencies. One of the most successful splinters of Santee Sioux was the colony started at Flandreau, South Dakota, in 1869 by twelve families who left Niobrara without permission to live on their own land like white men. By 1900, aided by missionary John Williamson, they had succeeded pretty well as farmers. They also earned additional income by fashioning pipes and other desirable items from the catlinite of nearby Pipestone Quarry in Minnesota. Among those who left the Nebraska reservation to settle at Flandreau in 1869 was Chief Big Eagle, who had been released from prison near Davenport. He later returned to the Minnesota River Valley to live near the site of the Upper Agency at Granite Falls, where he died in 1906.

The development of a new community near the old Lower Sioux Agency was spurred by the return of Chief Good Thunder, a Christian Sioux who had helped protect white settlers during the war even though he was reportedly present at the second battle of Fort Ridgely. In 1884 he bought eighty acres of land across the river from the old Birch Coulee battle site. Other Indians followed his lead. In 1886 the Reverend Hinman, at the request of Bishop Whipple, resumed the mission work at the Lower Agency that had been interrupted almost twenty-four years earlier by the uprising. Good Thunder offered to provide twenty acres of land for the erection of a house of worship. The resulting St. Cornelia's Episcopal Church, named for the wife of Bishop Whipple, was consecrated on July 15, 1891, and still stands as the center of the Lower Sioux community.

Thus small but significant numbers of Dakota returned to Minnesota in spite of their banishment "forever." Their long agony in prisons and on reservations did not destroy their pride in Dakota traditions nor did it totally obliterate the many cultural elements and crafts which remain a valued part of their heritage today.

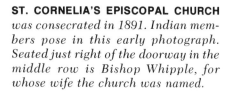

16.

THE KILLING OF LITTLE CROW

A HORSE-STEALING FORAY *of the type that Little Crow was engaged in when he met death is depicted here. Citizens from Cleveland, Minnesota, are shown surprising horse thieves near German Lake in Le Sueur County.* DRAWING BY W. H. CHILDS FROM *Leslie's Illustrated Newspaper,* SEPTEMBER 5, 1863.

CONSPICUOUSLY absent from the trials and punishment of the Sioux in 1862 was the leader of the uprising, Little Crow. After the battle of Wood Lake he fled to the Dakota prairies. With about 150 followers, he is believed to have wintered near Devils Lake in present-day northeastern North Dakota.

Early in 1863, accompanied by about sixty braves, he went to Fort Garry, now Winnipeg, where he got some provisions. The chief pleaded in vain, however, for Canadian intercession to obtain the release of the Sioux held prisoner in Minnesota. Little Crow returned to the state in June, 1863, on a horse-stealing foray. With him went sixteen men, a squaw, and his son, sixteen-year-old Wowinapa (or The Appearing One).

During June and early July several murders were committed in the Big Woods area, where warriors of Little Crow's party were operating. Among the victims were Captain John S. Cady, leader of a detachment of the Eighth Minnesota Regiment, which was ambushed on June 11, 1863, near Lake Elizabeth in Kandiyohi County; four members of the Amos W. Dustin family, killed while moving in an open wagon from one part of Wright County to another; and James A. McGannon, shot on July 1 near Fairhaven in southeastern Stearns

THE SHOOTING OF LITTLE CROW *near Hutchinson on July 3, 1863, is depicted in the sketch above. A bronze tablet on a boulder now marks the site of the Sioux chief's hapless death.* FROM CONNOLLY, *Minnesota Massacre.*

County. Whether Little Crow's braves were guilty of all these murders is not definitely known.

For Little Crow himself, the raid into Minnesota ended in tragedy. On the evening of July 3, according to various and sometimes contradictory stories, the chief and his son were picking berries some six miles northwest of Hutchinson. They were seen by two residents of McLeod County — Nathan Lamson and his son Chauncey — who were out hunting. Although the Lamsons did not know who the Indians were, they attacked them. Unseen by Little Crow and his son, Nathan Lamson crept up behind a tree close to the berry patch and shot the chief just above the hip. Before Lamson could retreat to cover, Little Crow returned the fire, slightly wounding his assailant in the shoulder. The farmer immediately dropped to the ground, crawled out of the line of fire, and attempted to reload his rifle. At that instant, Chauncey and Little Crow exchanged shots. The Sioux chief fell mortally wounded by a ball that penetrated his breast.

Thinking that his father was dead and fearing other Indians might be near, Chauncey hurried to Hutchinson for help. There several citizens and soldiers from the fort organized a party and, led by Lamson's youngest son, Birney, set out to investigate. As daylight broke, they reached the site of the shootings and found the body of an Indian, neatly laid out with a pair of new moccasins and the murdered McGannon's coat on or near it. The only sign of the elder Lamson was his discarded white shirt. When members of the party returned to Hutchinson, he was among the first to greet them. Lamson explained that he had waited quietly until the Indians' moaning and talking ceased. He then slipped away to town after nightfall.

84

LITTLE CROW, *the Sioux leader in the uprising, was killed in 1863 by Nathan and Chauncey Lamson while picking berries near Hutchinson.* PHOTO BY A. Z. SHINDLER, 1858; UNITED STATES BUREAU OF ETHNOLOGY, SMITHSONIAN INSTITUTION.

WOWINAPA *was Little Crow's son by the third of his six wives. The boy, who saw his father killed, stayed by him and gave him a drink of water before he died. In later life, Wowinapa became a Christian and took the name Thomas Wakeman. He is known as the founder of the YMCA among the Sioux.* PHOTO BY WHITNEY, 1864.

The dead Indian was taken to Hutchinson, where the scalp was removed and the corpse mutilated before it was buried disgracefully in a pile of offal. Several persons who saw the body declared it to be that of Little Crow. When their statements were ridiculed, these people pointed out that the corpse had a double set of teeth and displaced wristbones on both arms just as Little Crow had. The death of the chief was not positively confirmed until twenty-six days after the shooting when the half-starved Wowinapa, who had stayed with his father until he died and then fled, was captured by Sibley's soldiers near Devils Lake. The boy readily told them how the white men had shot Little Crow near Hutchinson.

Wowinapa was tried by a military commission and found guilty of participation in the uprising and of attempted murder and horse stealing. Though sentenced to be hanged, he eventually was released. In 1864 Nathan Lamson received from the state five hundred dollars as a reward for killing Little Crow, who had become the symbol of Indian resistance to white authority. Chauncey, who actually fired the fatal shot, collected a bounty on Little Crow's scalp.

A state monument erected near Hutchinson in 1929 marks the site of the demise of the chief who led the uprising. In 1971, some 109 years after his death, Little Crow received a decidedly delayed but more fitting burial when some of his bones that had long been held by the Minnesota Historical Society were returned to his family. The remains were buried at Flandreau in a simple, dignified ceremony attended by relatives of the chief, including his grandson Jesse Wakeman (the son of Wowinapa) who was then eighty-eight years of age. "We did not want any publicity on the burial," said Jesse. ". . . We decided Ta-o-ya-te-dutah [*Little Crow*] would be buried among his own with only his own on hand."

CHAUNCEY *(left) and* NATHAN LAMSON *(right), a father and son who were refugees at Hutchinson, shot Little Crow. Shortly after Wowinapa identified his father's body, Chauncey collected a bounty of seventy-five dollars from the state for the Sioux chief's scalp.*

CAMP POPE *near Redwood Falls was the starting point for Sibley's 1863 expedition to the Missouri River. Some 3,300 men gathered at the camp. A train of 225 wagons was required to carry the supplies for the march.* FROM CONNOLLY, *Minnesota Massacre.*

17.
SEQUEL
TO THE
1862 UPRISING

"THE SIOUX war may be considered at an end," wrote Pope to Henry W. Halleck, general in chief at Washington, on October 9, 1862. Thirteen days later Governor Ramsey informed President Lincoln that the conflict was "virtually closed."

In Minnesota the reaction to these statements was immediate. From several parts of the state came shouts that a definite Indian threat still remained. The Democratic press charged that Pope and Ramsey had made the announcements only to forestall a move by the administration to replace Pope as department commander with a civilian, Senator Henry M. Rice of Minnesota, whose term was about to expire.

Pope and Ramsey soon made it clear that they had no intention of removing all the troops from the frontier, as many panicky Minnesotans feared. Even though there was a great need for soldiers in the South, Pope said that he would send only the Third regiment to fight in the Civil War. The remaining five regiments would be retained at home, he said, "to restore confidence to a people panic-stricken at the awful outrages but recently perpetrated by the Sioux."

As distributed by Sibley, now commander of the Military District of Minnesota, the troops garrisoned numerous posts in two crescent-shaped defense lines from Fort Abercrombie east and south to the Iowa border. (See map pages 46–47.) Headquarters for the Sixth, Seventh, Eighth, Ninth, and Tenth regiments were, respectively, at Fort Snelling, Mankato, Fort Ripley, Fort Ridgely, and Le Sueur, with individual companies stationed at posts elsewhere. The soldiers patrolled designated areas daily to guard against Indian raids and prevent whites from plundering deserted settlements.

While defense measures were being reorganized in Minnesota, some eight hundred Lower Sioux and perhaps four thousand Upper Sioux roamed about Dakota Territory. The latter left their villages near Lakes Traverse and Big Stone because they had little faith in Sibley's promise

of safety if they surrendered. Also on the plains were thousands of Yankton and Yanktonai, who were thought to have joined the Minnesota Sioux still at large.

General Pope was convinced that these Indians would attack the Minnesota frontier during the coming summer. He therefore decided early in 1863 to send a two-pronged punitive expedition into Dakota Territory. One column, led by Sibley, was to be made up largely of infantry; it would march northward from near Fort Ridgely to the Devils Lake area. The other would be a cavalry unit headed by General Alfred Sully, who had fought in Civil War battles in the East. Sully would move up the Missouri River Valley from Fort Randall and then meet Sibley near Devils Lake. The Indians, it was hoped, would be caught in this pincers movement.

THIS MAP *shows the routes of military expeditions in Dakota Territory in 1863–64.* MAP BY ALAN OMINSKY.

In June, 1863, Sibley concentrated about 3,300 men at Camp Pope, near present-day Redwood Falls. The chief units represented in his command were the Sixth, Seventh, and Tenth regiments, the First Minnesota Mounted Rangers, and the Third Battery of Light Artillery commanded by Captain Jones, the hero of Fort Ridgely. In addition there were a hundred men from the Ninth Minnesota and seventy Indian and mixed-blood scouts. The Eighth regiment stayed at home to guard settlers and protect the all-important supply line between St. Cloud and Fort Abercrombie from such posts as Sauk Centre, Alexandria, and Pomme de Terre.

As Sibley's expedition moved out from Camp Pope on June 16 it formed a column five miles long. Over two hundred wagons carried enough provisions for ninety days. After a month's march, made tedious by dusty prairies, alkaline lakes, locusts, and heat, the command reached a point about forty miles southeast of Devils Lake, where a field base called Camp Atchison was established. Learning that six hundred lodges of Sioux had left Devils Lake and were heading toward the Missouri River, Sibley prepared to take out after them.

Early on July 20 about 2,300 men set out from the base camp, and four days later Sibley's scouts reported many Indians on the prairie and a large encampment not far distant. Sibley halted the column, and while camp was set up many Sioux watched from a range of hills about a mile away. A sizable group was stationed on the summit of the highest peak, called Big Mound, in what is now Kidder County, North Dakota. Some of these rode toward Sibley's camp — not, as the general hoped, in a show of friendship, but to warn him of the Indians' intention to fight. The battle of Big Mound was suddenly touched off when a young Indian, unmindful of the consequences, shot Dr. Josiah S. Weiser, surgeon of the Mounted Rangers. The outnumbered Indians (some 1,500 of them) fought until late afternoon before giving up the battle and retreating westward.

The Sioux were similarly routed in encounters at nearby Dead Buffalo Lake on July 26 and two days later at Stony Lake northeast of present-day Driscoll, North Dakota, where, Sibley reported, "there took place the greatest conflict between our troops and the Indians,

GENERAL ALFRED SULLY, *an experienced army man who had earlier served as colonel of the First Minnesota, led expeditions against the Sioux in Dakota Territory in 1863, 1864, and 1865.* FROM A TINTYPE TAKEN IN THE 1860s.

so far as the numbers were concerned." In each instance, Sibley's soldiers fought not against a war party but against a body of hunters whose major concern was to delay the expedition while their women and children crossed the Missouri River to safety. Although only one soldier was killed in all the battles, Sibley estimated the Sioux deaths at from 120 to 150. The Indians also suffered great losses of utensils and equipment in their hasty retreats.

On July 29, the day following the fight at Stony Lake, Sibley's command reached the Missouri's eastern bank. There, in the vicinity of present-day Bismarck, North Dakota, he waited for General Sully. Two days passed without a sign of Sully and, because his supplies were running low, Sibley decided to return home. His main column reached Fort Snelling on September 13.

Sully, delayed by low water in the Missouri and other difficulties, had not left his advance base near Fort Pierre (South Dakota) until August 21. About a week later he reached the Bismarck area and learned that Sibley's forces were on their way back to Minnesota. He then turned to the southeast to track down some Sioux hunting near the headwaters of the James River. After three days of rapid marching, his troops arrived at Whitestone Hill, now a North Dakota state park. There one of his forward battalions suddenly came upon a large group of unsuspecting Indians and immediately formed a battle line. The main force of the expedition came up about two hours later and found the Indians breaking camp. Sully ordered his men to advance and charge through the center of the Indians, who made a "very desperate resistance." Darkness put an end to the engagement, in which Sully lost twenty killed and thirty-eight wounded. He set the Indian losses at between 150 and 200, including women and children.

THE CAVALRY *of Sully's brigade charged the Sioux forces at the battle of Whitestone Hill on September 3, 1863. Sully successfully routed the Indians in this brief encounter. The site in North Dakota is appropriately marked.* FROM AN OFFICER'S SKETCH OF THE BATTLE IN *Harper's Weekly,* OCTOBER 31, 1863.

On November 13, 1863, Samuel J. Brown, nineteen-year-old interpreter at the Crow Creek agency on the Missouri, wrote a letter to his father, Joseph R. Brown, that presents the Indian side of Whitestone Hill and puts something of a cloud over Sully's victory. "I don't think he ought to brag of it at all," wrote Samuel, "because it was, what no decent man would have done, he pitched into their camp and just slaughtered them, worse a great deal than what the Indians did in 1862, he killed *very few* men and took *no* hostile ones prisoners, he *took* some but they were friendly Yanktons, and he let them go again . . . it is lamentable to hear how those women and children were slaughtered it was a perfect massacre, and now he returns saying that we need fear no more, for he has 'wiped out all hostile Indians from Dakota,' if he had killed men instead of women & children, then it would have been a success, and the worse of it, they had no hostile intention whatever . . ."

For two days following the battle of Whitestone Hill the expedition spread over the countryside destroying everything the enemy had abandoned, dispersing small bands of Indians, and capturing others. Sully returned to his base on the Missouri with 156 Sioux men, women, and children as prisoners. The 1863 expeditions had driven the main body of Sioux farther from the Minnesota border but had failed to kill or capture many of the Indians' fighting men. It was not long before the Dakota were again back across the Missouri hunting buffalo.

General Sully led another expedition to Dakota Territory in 1864. He marched up the Missouri Valley with a brigade that included one Minnesota unit, Brackett's battalion of cavalry. On June 28, he was joined by a second brigade from Minnesota under Colonel Minor T. Thomas of the Eighth Minnesota. In addition to that regiment, Thomas' force included part of the Second Minnesota cavalry and two sections of Captain Jones's Third Minnesota Battery. The combined brigades, about 2,200 men, crossed the river and established Fort Rice on its western bank in present North Dakota.

The climax of this expedition came at Killdeer Mountain, southeast of present-day Watford City in northwestern North Dakota. There on July 28 Indians from an estimated sixteen hundred lodges watched as the soldiers approached. The Sioux apparently were confident of victory, for their women and children had come out to witness the battle that followed. No match for the experienced and well-equipped soldiers, the Indians fought hard but with little success until sunset. Then they joined their women and children and fled, leaving behind lodges, food, utensils, and even some dogs and horses. Five of Sully's men were killed and ten wounded. The Indian loss was thought to be from 100 to 150. Following the battle at Killdeer Mountain, the expedition pressed westward through the Badlands to the Yellowstone River and then turned toward home. On October 8, after having marched 1,625 miles, the Minnesota brigade arrived at Fort Ridgely. Further marches were made into Dakota Territory by the military in 1865, but no Sioux were encountered.

Occasional Indian marauders still broke through the cordon of posts and patrols to create panic along the Minnesota frontier. A case in point was the murder of four members of the Andrew J. Jewett family on May 2, 1865, near Garden City in Blue Earth County. As a result, a mob at Mankato lynched John L. Campbell, a mixed-blood, who had been convicted of the crime. Some forts in the state were garrisoned as late as 1866, but gradually the Indian raids ceased, and settlers slowly began to filter back into the wide area depopulated by the Sioux Uprising.

In a broader sense, however, the Sioux War went on for many years. As the frontier moved westward, other Dakota tribes rose against the white man. Little Crow and the Minnesota Uprising of 1862 were still fresh in the nation's memory when it became aware of such Indian leaders as Red Cloud, Sitting Bull, and Crazy Horse. Bloody battles at Fort Phil Kearny, the Little Bighorn, and, in 1890, Wounded Knee, brought to an end at last the generation of Indian warfare that had begun at Acton in August, 1862.

THE BATTLE OF KILLDEER MOUNTAIN *in North Dakota, which was fought by Sully's troops on July 28, 1864, successfully scattered the Sioux.* OIL BY CARL L. BOECKMANN IN THE MINNESOTA CAPITOL.

THE LITERATURE of the Sioux Uprising and its aftermath is extensive and frequently contradictory. Below are listed selected works consulted in the preparation of this narrative. The most useful were the second volume of William W. Folwell's *A History of Minnesota*, the two volumes of *Minnesota in the Civil and Indian Wars, 1861–1865*, and the various *Minnesota Historical Society Collections* cited.

PRINTED MATERIALS

Adams, Moses N. "The Sioux Outbreak in the Year 1862, With Notes of Missionary Work Among the Sioux," in *Minnesota Historical Society Collections*, v. 9, p. 431–452. St. Paul, 1901.

"Condemned Sioux Humanized After 110 Years," in *Mankato Free Press*, December 26, 1972, p. 25. [Reproduces 10 drawings by Robert O. Sweeny and confessions and evidence against the pictured Indians.]

Andrist, Ralph K. *The Long Death: The Last Days of the Plains Indian.* New York, 1964. [Pages 27–68 comprise a readable chapter entitled "Massacre in Minnesota."]

———— "Massacre!" in *American Heritage*, v. 13, p. 8–17 (April, 1962). [Brief account illustrated by reproductions from John Stevens' panorama.]

Babcock, Willoughby M. "Minnesota's Frontier: A Neglected Sector of the Civil War," in *Minnesota History*, v. 38, p. 274–286 (June, 1963). [Army and militia movements and frontier forts in the Sioux War.]

———— "Minnesota's Indian War," in *Minnesota History*, v. 38, p. 93–98 (September, 1962). [This brief account of the war, 100 years after, was part of a special issue of the quarterly, now out of print.]

Bean, Geraldine. "General Alfred Sully and the Northwest Indian Expedition," in *North Dakota History*, v. 33, p. 240-259 (Summer, 1966).

Bishop [McConkey], Harriet E. *Dakota War Whoop: Or, Indian Massacres and War in Minnesota, of 1862-'63.* Minneapolis, 1970. [Reprint of 1864 edition of one of the earliest accounts of the war, with foreword by Kenneth Carley.]

Blegen, Theodore C. "Guri Endreson, Frontier Heroine," in *Minnesota History*, v. 10, p. 425–430 (December, 1929).

Board of Commissioners. *Minnesota in the Civil and Indian Wars, 1861–1865.* St. Paul, 1890, 1899. 2 v. [Includes regimental histories, reports, orders, rosters, and other important documents dealing with the uprising. The narratives of Charles E. Flandrau and Thomas P. Gere were especially useful.]

Boyd, Robert K. *The Battle of Birch Coulee.* Eau Claire, Wis., 1925. [A pamphlet containing an account of the battle by a participant.]

Brown, Dee A. *Bury My Heart at Wounded Knee: An Indian History of the American West.* New York, 1970. [The third chapter, p. 37–65, entitled "Little Crow's War" presents the Indians' viewpoint.]

Brown, Samuel J. *In Captivity.* Mankato, 1900. [A pamphlet on the captivity of the author and others. Also published in 56 Congress, 2 session, *Senate Document*, no. 23 — serial 4029.]

Bryant, Charles S. and Abel B. Murch. *A History of the Great Massacre by the Sioux Indians in Minnesota.* Cincinnati, 1864. [Contains many narratives by captives, but must be used with caution.]

Buck, Daniel. *Indian Outbreaks.* Mankato, 1904; reprint edition, Minneapolis, 1965.

Buell, Salmon A. "Judge Flandrau in the Defense of New Ulm During the Sioux Outbreak of 1862," in *Minnesota Historical Society Collections*, v. 10, part 2, p. 783–818. St. Paul, 1905.

Carley, Kenneth. "As Red Men Viewed It: Three Indian Accounts of the Uprising," in *Minnesota History*, v. 38, p. 126–149 (September, 1962). [Story of Big Eagle in new edited version, plus those of Lightning Blanket and George Quinn.]

———— "The Sioux Campaign of 1862: Sibley's Letters to His Wife," in *Minnesota History*, v. 38, p. 99–114 (September, 1962).

Christianson, Theodore. *Minnesota, the Land of Sky-Tinted Waters: A History of the State and Its People.* Chicago and New York, 1935. 5 v. [Chapters 16 and 17 of volume 1 deal with the uprising and its aftermath.]

Clapesattle, Helen B. *The Doctors Mayo.* Minneapolis, 1941. [Pages 68–78 concern Dr. William W. Mayo's role in the uprising.]

Connolly, A. P. *A Thrilling Narrative of the Minnesota Massacre and the Sioux War of 1862–63.* Chicago, 1896.

Connors, Joseph. "The Elusive Hero of Redwood Ferry," in *Minnesota History*, v. 34, p. 233–238 (Summer, 1955). [A thorough account of the ferryman in the war.]

Curtiss-Wedge, Franklyn. *The History of Redwood County, Minnesota.* Chicago, 1916. 2 v. [Pages 88–167 of volume 1 were especially useful.]

Daniels, Asa W. "Reminiscences of Little Crow," in *Minnesota Historical Society Collections*, v. 12, p. 513–630. St. Paul, 1908.

———— "Reminiscences of the Little Crow Uprising," in *Minnesota Historical Society Collections*, v. 15, p. 323–336. St. Paul, 1915.

Danziger, Edmund J., Jr. "The Crow Creek Experiment: An Aftermath of the Sioux War of 1862," in *North Dakota History*, v. 37, p. 104–123 (Spring, 1970).

———— *Indians and Bureaucrats: Administering the Reservation Policy during the Civil War.* Urbana, Ill., 1974. [Pages 95–130 tell the story of "The Uprooted Santees."]

Davis, Jane S. "Two Sioux War Orders: A Mystery Unraveled," in *Minnesota History*, v. 41, p. 117–[125] (Fall, 1968).

Dietz, Charlton. "Henry Behnke: New Ulm's Paul Revere," in *Minnesota History*, v. 45, p. 111–115 (Fall, 1976).

Edgerton, Jay. "Minnesota's War: The Sioux Outbreak," in *Gopher Reader*, v. 1, p. 26–28. St. Paul, 1958.

Ellis, Richard N. "Political Pressures and Army Policies on the Northern Plains, 1862–1865," in *Minnesota History*, v. 42, p. 42–53 (Summer, 1970). [How excitement in Minnesota affected later army campaigns in the West.]

Flandrau, Charles E. "The Ink-pa-du-ta Massacre of 1857," in *Minnesota Historical Society Collections*, v. 3, p. 386–407. St. Paul, 1880.

Folwell, William W. *A History of Minnesota.* St. Paul, 1921–1930. 4 v. Reprint editions of volumes 1 and 2, 1956, 1961. [Volume 2 of this work contains the best account of the uprising yet written.]

Fridley, Russell W. "Charles E. Flandrau: Attorney at War," in *Minnesota History*, v. 38, p. 116–125 (September, 1962). [An able assessment of Flandrau's role in defeating the Sioux.]

————, Leota M. Kellett, and June D. Holmquist, eds. *Charles E. Flandrau and the Defense of New Ulm.* New Ulm, 1962; reprint edition, 1976.

Fritsche, Louis A., ed. *History of Brown County, Minnesota.* Indianapolis, Ind., 1916. 2 v. [Volume 1, chapter 5 contains numerous reminiscences of the uprising.]

Gilman, Rhoda R. "The Fur Trade in the Upper Mississippi Valley, 1630–1850," in *Wisconsin Magazine of History*, v. 58, p. 2–18 (Autumn, 1974). [Good for background on the Sioux and other Indians over a long period before the 1862 war.]

Gluek, Alvin C., Jr., "The Sioux Uprising: A Problem in International Relations," in *Minnesota History*, v. 34, p. 317–324 (Winter, 1955).

Gray, John S. "The Santee Sioux and the Settlers at Lake Shetek," in *Montana the Magazine of Western History*, v. 25, p. 42–54 (Winter, 1975). [The captivity and rescue of some Shetek survivors.]

Heard, Isaac V. D. *History of the Sioux War and Massacres of 1862 and 1863.* New York, 1863. [In spite of its many errors, this is a significant source because of its first-hand observations by a lawyer who acted as recorder at the Sioux trials.]

Heilbron, Bertha L. *The Thirty-Second State: A Pictorial History of Minnesota.* St. Paul, 1958; 2nd edition, 1966. [Chapter 15 gives a good, illustrated summary of the Sioux War.]

Henig, Gerald S. "A Neglected Cause of the Sioux Uprising," in *Minnesota History*, v. 45, p. 107–110 (Fall, 1976).

Holcombe, Return I., ed. "A Sioux Story of the War: Chief Big Eagle's Story of the Sioux Outbreak of 1862," in *Minnesota Historical Society Collections*, v. 6, p. 382–400. St. Paul, 1894. [The best account of the uprising from the Indian viewpoint.]

Holmquist, June D. and Jean A. Brookins. *Minnesota's Major Historic Sites: A Guide.* Revised edition, St. Paul, 1972. [See especially pages 121–137 and the list of Minnesota state monuments, p. 179, 180].

Hubbard, Lucius F. and Return I. Holcombe. *Minnesota in Three Centuries, 1655–1908.* Mankato, 1908. 4 v. [Volume 3, chapters 11–28, gives an extended account of the uprising.]

Hughes, Thomas. "Causes and Results of the Inkpaduta Massacre," in *Minnesota Historical Society Collections*, v. 12, p. 263–282. St. Paul, 1908.

———— *Indian Chiefs of Southern Minnesota.* Mankato, 1927; reprint edition, Minneapolis, 1969. [Useful biographical sketches of prominent Sioux leaders in the uprising.]

———— "The Treaty of Traverse des Sioux in 1851," in *Minnesota Historical Society Collections*, v. 10, part 1, p. 101–129. St. Paul, 1905.

Humphrey, John A. "Boyhood Remembrances of Life Among the Dakotas and the Massacre in 1862," in *Minnesota Historical Society Collections*, v. 15, p. 337–348. St. Paul, 1915.

Johnson, Roy P. "The Siege at Fort Abercrombie," in *North Dakota History*, v. 24, p. 5–79 (January, 1957).

Jones, Robert H. *The Civil War in the Northwest: Nebraska, Wisconsin, Iowa, Minnesota, and the Dakotas.* Norman, Okla., 1960. [Emphasizes the role of General John Pope and the Department of the Northwest.]

Kane, Lucile M. "The Sioux Treaties and the Traders," in *Minnesota History*, v. 32, p. 65–80 (June, 1951).

Kappler, Charles J., comp. and ed. *Indian Affairs: Laws and Treaties.* Washington, D.C., 1904–29. 5 v. [Pertinent Sioux treaties may be found in volume 2, p. 588–593, 781–789.]

Kunz, Virginia B. *Muskets to Missiles: A Military History of Minnesota.* St. Paul, 1958. [Chapter 3 concerns "The Indian Wars."]

Lamson, Frank B. *Condensed History of Meeker County 1855–1939.* Litchfield, [1939].

Lass, William E. "The 'Moscow Expedition,'" in *Minnesota History*, v. 39, p. 227–241 (Summer, 1965).

———— "The Removal from Minnesota of the Sioux and Winnebago Indians," in *Minnesota History*, v. 38, p. 353–364 (December, 1963).

Lawson, Victor E. and Martin E. Tew, comps. *Illustrated History and Descriptive and Biographical Review of Kandiyohi County, Minnesota.* St. Paul, 1905. [The first twelve chapters concern the uprising.]

Lightning Blanket. "Indian Tells of Ridgely Battles," in *New Ulm Review*, August 22, 1917. [A Sioux warrior's account as told to R. H. Hinman.]

"Lincoln's Sioux War Order," in *Minnesota History*, v. 33, p. 77–79 (Summer, 1952).

McClure-Huggan, Nancy. "The Story of Nancy [Faribault] McClure," in *Minnesota Historical Society Collections*, v. 6, 439–460. St. Paul, 1894.

McKusick, Marshall. *The Iowa Northern Border Brigade.* Iowa City, 1975. [Chapters 2 and 6 deal with Minnesota aspects and aftermath of the uprising.]

———— "Major William Williams at Iowa Lake in 1862," in *Annals of Iowa*, v. 42, p. 569–582 (Spring, 1975).

[Matson, Cynthia A.]. *Fort Ridgely: A Journal of the Past.* St. Paul, 1972. [Newspaper format. Discusses the Ridgely battles and other aspects of the frontier fort.]

Meyer, Roy W. "The Canadian Sioux: Refugees from Minnesota," in *Minnesota History*, v. 41, p. 13–28 (Spring, 1968).

———— "The Establishment of the Santee Reservation, 1866–1869," in *Nebraska History*, v. 45, p. 59–97 (March, 1964).

———— *History of the Santee Sioux: United States Indian Policy on Trial.* Lincoln, Neb., 1967. [A good general history of the Santee that includes considerable information on the war in Minnesota.]

Minnesota Executive Documents, 1862. St. Paul, 1863. [Alexander Ramsey's message to the 1862 legislature and the valuable report of the adjutant general may be found on pages 3–553.]

Newcombe, Barbara T. "A Portion of the American People: The Sioux Sign a Treaty in Washington in 1858," in *Minnesota History*, v. 45, p. 82–96 (Fall, 1976).

Nichols, David A. "The Other Civil War: Lincoln and the Indians," in *Minnesota History*, v. 44, p. 2–15 (Spring, 1974).

Nicolay, John G. "The Sioux War," in Theodore C. Blegen, ed., *Lincoln's Secretary Goes West: Two Reports by John G. Nicolay on Frontier Indian Troubles 1862.* La Crosse, Wis., 1965. [An account of Nicolay's trip to Minnesota first published in *Continental Monthly*, v. 3, p. 195–204 (February, 1863).]

Oehler, C. M. *The Great Sioux Uprising.* New York, 1959. [Emphasizes the lurid stories of settlers caught in the uprising.]

Olson, Aslak. "Story Told of Acton Killing," in *Litchfield Independent*, September 25, 1912. [Relates Mrs. Howard Baker's version of the Acton story.]

Pendergast, William W. "Sketches of the History of Hutchinson," in *Minnesota Historical Society Collections*, v. 10, part 1, p. 78–89. St. Paul, 1905.

Pfaller, Louis. "Sully's Expedition of 1864, featuring the Killdeer Mountain and Badlands Battles," in *North Dakota History*, v. 31, p. 25–77 (January, 1964).

Randall, Benjamin H. "Siege of Fort Ridgely, August, 1862," in *Winona Republican*, March 5, 1892.

Renville, Gabriel. "A Sioux Narrative of the Outbreak in 1862, and of Sibley's Expedition in 1863," in *Minnesota Historical Society Collections*, v. 10, part 2, p. 595–618. St. Paul, 1905.

Riggs, Stephen R. *Mary and I: Forty Years With the Sioux.* Chicago, 1880; Boston, 1887; reprint edition, Minneapolis, 1969.

———— "Memoir of Hon. James W. Lynd," in *Minnesota Historical Society Collections*, v. 3, p. 107–114. St. Paul, 1880.

———— trans. "Narrative of Paul Mazakootemane," in *Minnesota Historical Society Collections*, v. 3, p. 82–90. St. Paul, 1880.

Robinson, Doane. *A History of the Dakota or Sioux Indians.* Aberdeen, S.D., 1904; reprint edition, Minneapolis, 1956.

Roddis, Louis H. *The Indian Wars of Minnesota.* Cedar Rapids, Ia., 1956. [Stresses military operations in connection with the uprising.]

Rose, Arthur P. *An Illustrated History of Yellow Medicine County, Minnesota.* Marshall, 1914. [Chapters 2, 3, 4, and 20 were useful.]

Russo, Priscilla Ann. "The Time to Speak Is Over: The Onset of the Sioux Uprising," in *Minnesota History*, v. 45, p. 97–106 (Fall, 1976).

Satterlee, Marion P. *A Detailed Account of the Massacre by the Dakota Indians of Minnesota in 1862.* Minneapolis, 1923.

———— "Narratives of the Sioux War," *Minnesota Historical Society Collections*, v. 15, p. 349–370. St. Paul, 1915.

———— *The Story of Capt. Richard Strout and Company.* [Minneapolis, 1909].

Schwandt-Schmidt, Mary. "The Story of Mary Schwandt," in *Minnesota Historical Society Collections*, v. 6, p. 461–474. St. Paul, 1894.

Smith, Abner C. *A Random Historical Sketch of Meeker County.* Litchfield, 1877.

Smith, G. Hubert. "A Frontier Fort in Peacetime," in *Minnesota History*, v. 45, p. 116–128 (Fall, 1976). [A study of Fort Ridgely before the war.]

Snana. "Narration of a Friendly Sioux," in *Minnesota Historical Society Collections*, v. 9, p. 427–430. St. Paul, 1901.

Spavin, Don. "Little Crow: Dacotah Chief Finds Peace at Last," in *Capital*, Sunday magazine of *St. Paul Pioneer Press*, November 7, 1971, p. 7–9, 18, 19. [An account of the 1971 funeral at Flandreau, S. Dak.]

Sully, Langdon. *No Tears for the General: The Life of Alfred Sully, 1821–1879.* Palo Alto, Cal., 1974. [Noncritical biography by grandson contains material on the Sioux War and "Battle of the Bad Lands" in chapter 9 and 10.]

Sweet, Jannette E. "Mrs. J. E. De Camp Sweet's Narrative of Her Captivity in the Sioux Outbreak of 1862," in *Minnesota Historical Society Collections*, v. 6, p. 354–380. St. Paul, 1894.

Trenerry, Walter N. "The Shooting of Little Crow: Heroism or Murder?" in *Minnesota History*, v. 38, p. 150–153 (September, 1962).

United States Office of Indian Affairs. *Report of the Commissioner, 1863.* Washington, D.C., 1864. [Thomas J. Galbraith's important report is on pages 266–298.]

United States War Department. *War of the Rebellion: A Compilation of the Official Records of the Union and Confederate Armies.* Washington, D.C., 1880–1901. Series 1, 70 v. [Volumes 13, 22, and 23 were useful for reports and correspondence concerning the uprising and its sequel.]

Utley, Robert M. *Frontiersmen in Blue: The United States Army and the Indian, 1848–1865.* New York, 1967. [Chapter 13 contains a good section on "Sibley, Sully, and the Sioux, 1862–64."]

Wakefield, Sarah F. *Six Weeks in the Sioux Tepees: A Narrative of Indian Captivity.* Shakopee, 1864.

Wall, Oscar G. *Recollections of the Sioux Massacre.* [Lake City], 1908. [Includes an account of William J. Sturgis' ride on pages 110–117.]

Webb, Wayne E. and Jasper I. Swedberg. *Redwood: The Story of a County.* [Redwood Falls], 1964. [Covers the Sioux War in a chapter called "Burning Path to Banishment," p. 75–116.]

West, Nathaniel. *The Ancestry, Life, and Times of Hon. Henry Hastings Sibley.* St. Paul, 1889.

Whipple, Henry B. *Lights and Shadows of a Long Episcopate.* New York, 1900.

White, Urania N. D. "Captivity Among the Sioux, August 18 to September 26, 1862," in *Minnesota Historical Society Collections*, v. 9, p. 395–426. St. Paul, 1901.

Woolworth, Alan R. "A Disgraceful Proceeding: Intrigue in the Red River Country in 1864," in *The Beaver*, Spring, 1969, p. 54–59. [How Little Six (Shakopee) and Medicine Bottle were "spirited" out of Canada.]

MANUSCRIPTS

All manuscripts cited are in the Division of Archives and Manuscripts, Minnesota Historical Society, unless otherwise noted.

Currie, Neil. Information on victims of the Sioux massacre at Lake Shetek.

Daniels, Jared W. A series of reminiscences on the Sioux Uprising. [Important observations of a doctor who was on the scene.]

Folwell, William W. Papers. Historical notes and correspondence on the Sioux War, 1862–63, on Joseph R. Brown, Inkpaduta, Fort Ridgely, New Ulm, and Wood Lake, gathered by Folwell in the course of preparing his *History of Minnesota.*

Gere, Thomas P. Papers. "A Scrap of Frontier History: Fort Ridgely," and a typed copy of a journal kept by Gere during the uprising.

Ives, Luther C. "Expedition of Leavenworth Company on August 19, 1862," a reminiscence owned by the Brown County Historical Society, New Ulm.

[Johnson, Jasper W.] "Fort Ridgely, Minnesota." [A lengthy and useful manuscript history of the fort.]

Jones, John. Papers, 1847–1937. [Included is a letter from Benjamin H. Randall to Jones, February 5, 1881, giving interesting details of the Fort Ridgely battles.]

Larson, Peggy. "Inkpaduta — Renegade Sioux." Master's thesis, Mankato State College, 1969. [A biography of the chief instigator of the Spirit Lake Massacre of 1857.]

Minnesota Governors' Archives, 1862–63. [Valuable files of official orders and correspondence for the period of the uprising.]

Oswald, Gottlieb C. "What I Remember of the Sioux Outbreak," a reminiscence in the possession of the Brown County Historical Society, New Ulm.

Pendergast, William W. Papers. "The Killing of Little Crow as told by Nathan and Chauncey Lamson."

Sibley, Henry H. Papers. [Correspondence and order books for the period of the uprising, 1862–63. Especially valuable are letters written by Sibley to his wife during the campaign.]

Smith, G. Hubert. "Historical Narrative for Fort Ridgely." [An informative report by the archaeologist who excavated the fort site.]

Stipe, Claude E. "Eastern Dakota Acculturation: The Role of Agents of Culture Change." Ph.D. thesis, University of Minnesota, 1968. [A study of the role of missionaries, fur traders, and government officials in effecting cultural change among the Santee.]

U. S. Senate. Records pertaining to Indian barbarities in the state of Minnesota. Microfilm copy (National Archives Record Group 46, 3 rolls) of original transcripts of U.S. Army Military Commission, Sioux War Trials, 1862, which accompanied President Lincoln's message to the Senate, December 11, 1862.

U. S. War Department. Photostats of orders and correspondence revealing troop movements during the uprising, copied from originals in the National Archives, Washington, D.C.

Walsh, Kenneth Lee. "A Biography of a Frontier Outpost — Fort Ridgely." Master's thesis, University of Minnesota, Duluth, 1957. [An account of the fort before and during the war.]